No Ordinary Woman
LS King

a BlackWyrm book
Louisville, Kentucky

NO ORDINARY WOMAN

A BlackWyrm Book
BlackWyrm Publishing
10307 Chimney Ridge Ct, Louisville, KY 40299

Printed in the United States of America.

ISBN: 978-1-61318-122-5
LCCN: 2011944765
Cover design by Dave Mattingly
Edited by Linda Mattingly

Second Edition: January 2012

Foreword

There are many examples of people who have created wonderful things as a result of painful experiences in their lives. Violet is a prime example. It was always her wish that her children know about her childhood. I can still remember listening to stories shared around our kitchen table and I was usually uninterested with these stories because they were so unrealistic compared to my knowledge of life experiences. Places, names and events were never important to any of us as children. Writing these stories at the age of somewhere over fifty, I long to have been a fly on the wall and revisit my mother as a child growing up in the 1900s. Why, were her friends and neighbors so important to her? I would soon find out as I promised to write her story for her family to read.

Reading her stories and visiting her hometown makes me appreciate my roots. How can we know how far we have come, if we don't realize where we have been? This has been an amazingly enriching experience. Violet enjoyed reading and writing. Every day, she wrote in her journal. She made sure that she recorded special events that took place. She was proud of her accomplishments and noted them in her journal. With no prior experience in formal education, she opened her own business. She loved children and learned to fight for children's issues in congress. She over stepped others who had less experience and more education in the field of early childhood. She gave speeches, and taught classes on building a business. She was a hero to many women in the fifties and the sixties. A role model to those women who were stay at home mom's trying to survive on their husband's small salary. She survived a broken marriage but she didn't let this destroy her zest for living. She had two children to raise and no money. It was a difficult time, but the opportunity was there and she made the most of her situation.

She embraced her early life when times were simple and life

offered new and exciting adventures.

She had survived the great depression and growing up poor without food and clothing. She knew how hard life could be and how brutal people could be. She learned early in life, that her happiness came from family. She longed for a happy family. She protected her children and knew that her goal in life was to shape her girls into women who could survive like she did. She knew how to control every situation and became preoccupied with controlling. She was a survivor and confident enough to face any task without the help or advice of a husband, friend or sibling. She earned the right to make her own decisions and spend her money without permission.

Later in Violet's life she fights for independence as her health keeps her captive in her home and hostage to mental abuse. Violet struggled to gain back the control she once had. Her personality changed. She lost all sense of self. She never accepted the fact that God was always in control. Violet was now eighty-five years old.

She had beat the odds and lived ten years with a diseased heart. She didn't want to face the reality that she would soon meet her maker. She had been a Christian for most of her life. She had faced all kinds of obstacle with faith and prayer. Now as death entered her mind. She doubted her relationship with God.

When you don't believe... When you give into your doubts and fears... you give up everything God has put inside of you. You miss the miracles that God has waiting for you. Violet was about to experience the wonderful journey of eternity. She was still looking for happiness in people and things. Happiness she couldn't find in her physical life.

Violet was caught up in the worldly day to day problems that our physical body experiences. We all know that Jesus loves us, but we get so involved with solving insignificant problems that we fail to acknowledge that Jesus loves everything about us. Let's not forget that through prayer and our communication with God on a daily basis, we can become truly and totally committed to our Lord Jesus Christ. With this total commitment and communication, God will show us that we have a purpose in life. He is in control of our life and will remain in control until the day we die. He is our loving savior who has made a promise to love us when everyone and everything has turned against us.

Violet was frustrated with her life. She was a wonderful person and a Godly person. She used the spiritual gifts that God gave her. She gave money to those in need, she taught Sunday school, she prayed for and with people, she cooked for the sick and shut-ins, she took in the poor, she took care of her family financially and physically. With all the wonderful things Violet shared, she never felt loved. Therefore, she couldn't give deep down unconditional love. She would never allow me to acknowledge this tidbit of information to anyone who reads this book. If there is an editor in heaven today, I am sure she would demand that he/she swoop down on my computer and eject the last few chapters from this book. The secret of her happiness is exposed. Life is not a fairy tale. Violet wanted to believe it was. She held on to the lie till the very end. Many of us are looking for the silver lining that life has promised us. In reality, life doesn't promise us a silver lining. God doesn't promise us a silver lining. He only promises that he will love us and that was the ingredients that Violet was desperately seeking.

I hope you enjoy reading about Violet. She was an inspiration to many and I hope she will be an inspiration to you. I learned that we pass our feelings of self worth down to our children and grandchildren. I am sure that my mother would not have shared all the facts concerning the last phase of her life. I think she would have written about the "happy family" she fantasized about. She would not have admitted her unhappiness. She would not have admitted that she was controlling, bitter, and depressed. She would however, tell everyone that she loved the Lord. I have to ask myself, "Why then was she so self-consumed and unhappy?" She never knew that the most important thing in life is the love exchange between God and you. His perfect love is goodness. While reading Violet's story, remember God loves you for who you are, not for what you do. Pass this message down to your children and tell them daily that God loves them.

Romans 8:39
Neither height nor depth, nor anything else in all creation, will be able to separate us from the love of God that is in Christ Jesus our Lord.

The Heart Attack

It was a warm autumn day. I was preoccupied with show and tell just like every other Tuesday morning. A kindergarten class full of noisy little children anxious to share what was carefully tucked away in backpacks was typical of the week activities. Show and tell always gave me a sense of joy. I was somehow contributing to one's self-confidence by applauding his/her ability to share in front of the class. As each child sits around the circle waiting for his/her name to be called, the public address system in my classroom turned on and I sat at attention waiting to hear a voice from the office. "Miss Stapleton, you have an important call and I think that you should take it in the principal's main office." Hearing the urgency, I left the class in the hands of my assistant and went straight to the office. I could hear my sister Janice's voice on the other end of the phone. She sounded frightened but confused.

She said, "Lyn, Mom's having chest pains and I think she should go to the hospital. She doesn't know that I am calling you, but it sounds serious."

I replied, "Why don't you just call 911 and take her to the hospital?"

Her voice sounded worried as Janice continued, "No! She wants to see Dr. Bently first. She's trying to get dressed to go to the doctor. You may want to get things together for a sub tomorrow." There was a pause and then Janice said "I really would like to have you here with me. Is there any way you could come home?"

"*Now*?" I asked.

Janice lingered for a moment, "Well I guess not. I'll call you later Sis."

Instead of saying goodbye, I replied, "Make her go to the hospital."

She whispered goodbye and placed the phone on the hook.

My body was numb as I returned to the classroom. How could

this be happening? What would I do without her? I had never spent one day without her in my life. How could I go on? I confided in the assistant teacher and she quickly took over the class while I gathered my thoughts. An hour passed and once again I was called to the office.

It was my sister. "The doctor says she's having a heart attack. She may not make it to the hospital if we don't act now. I am going to call the EMS, and I think you better come home right away. Meet me at Mom's." Immediately I rushed down the hall and was granted permission to leave school.

The EMS was arriving as I pulled up in the driveway. I watched as they put mom on the gurney and rolled her down the drive. What would life be like without her? She will never know how my life will play out. Why couldn't she wait until I was married? Will she ever know the children I hope to have someday? Why now? I realized I still needed her. As hard as it was for me to admit, I still needed her. My mom! The person that stands in the way when I try to capture adulthood. The woman that still calls me her baby. The woman that takes away my confidence. I hold her responsible for everything that I can and can't do. Why now? Could I exist on my own? All of these questions were running wild in my brain as Janice and I drove quietly to the hospital behind the flashing red light of the emergency medical vehicle.

For two weeks we were held captive in the small waiting room outside the ICU of Southwest Hospital. The news was worse than we expected. She suffered two major heart attacks that day.

The heart was damaged beyond repair and things looked grim. We were all in shock. The doctor called the family together to give us a final analysis of what we could expect in the future. He related, "I can't operate on her, but I can try some new medicines that will open up small blood vessels and allow the heart to transport blood. I can't say how long it will last or how much time she has. I can only tell you to take it day by day. She needs lots of rest and will have to learn to live life at a slower pace." The words of the doctor rang in my ears as I looked around the room at my family, each with their husbands and children. I cried and prayed a lot that night. The next day before I visited the ICU unit, I visited the chapel in the hospital. I prayed that God would somehow hear my prayer and save my mom. I needed to tell her so many things. I needed to prove myself. I always wanted her to see me as a successful woman. A woman with a career, a home, and a family. I pleaded with God to let her live. I asked for a miracle.

As I made my way back to the ICU unit I heard a sweet voice call over the intercom,

"Is Violet's daughter out there?"

"Yes!" I said, with great delight.

The nurse replied, "Would you like to come back and feed her, she says she's hungry."

I didn't give a response. I bounced through the doors and found my mom sitting up in bed for the first time in weeks. God gave me the miracle I had asked for. Each day she grew stronger and so did I. Her strong will to live gave her one more chance to tell the entire world about her life, and thus she sat down to write her life's story for her children and grandchildren.

Believe, and your impossibilities become possible.

Mark 9:23
Jesus said, "Everything is possible for him who believes."

The Very Beginning

Violet Theona Beanblossom was born on January 12, 1918. She was born at home in the small town of Dogwood, Indiana. Dogwood is a town located in southern Harrison Indiana between Corydon and Laconia. It is one of the smallest towns in Harrison County, having an area of thirty square miles and a population of eighteen families. Violet's great, great grandfather was one of the first settlers of the area. Joseph Eckart came to the valley in 1812. He settled on the lower rich bottom land next to the south fork of Buck Creek. Violet's mother was Bessie Eckart who married Ona Arthur Beanblossom. Ona grew up in Mauckport a small river town close to Dogwood. Bessie and Ona was a young couple in their twenties. They lived in Dogwood on a farm they rented from Ona's cousin Curry. Bessie came from a family of five children. She loved her siblings but was happy to marry and get away from home. Bessie and Ona looked forward to farming the land and raising a family. After two years of marriage, they were now expecting their first child.

Life was hard on the farm. Daily chores were much harder to perform being nine months pregnant. There was no way Bessie could have guessed what was in store for her as she lay on the bed to rest her bulging body awaiting the new addition to their family.

Ona looked tenderly at his wife and said, "Bessie, is everything alright?"

She placed his hands on the baby and he could feel the rapid movement of the abdomen. "I sure hope you don't have that baby today. It's beginning to snow and the chill in the air will knock you down."

Looking a little anxious, she replied "Now Ona, you know I don't have a say over when this baby is coming. It just may be here today the way I feel."

As they lay there watching the movement of the baby, Bessie

started thinking about the weather. What if there was a real snow storm moving in on their small town. What would she do? She started giving it more thought and then gave Ona instructions. "Maybe you better call on my brother Frank and see if you two can plow a path with the horses. If it continues to snow like this, the doctor won't be able to get here from town."

Ona got up and walked over to the chair to retrieve his coat and hat.

Giving it one last thought, Bessie grabbed his hand and continued with instructions. "It wouldn't hurt to go across the road and call Violet Letchol. She's a nurse. She'll know what to do."

Ona looked worried, "Bessie, are you sure you'll be okay here by yourself?"

She gave a quick nod and replied, "I think it's going to be a long night. Hurry back."

As Violet Letchol (Bessie's best friend) entered the door of the small farmhouse she saw that Bessie's breathing showed early stages of labor. Violet walked over to the side of the bed. She held Bessie's hand and knew that she was definitely in a lot of pain. Sitting down beside her best friend, she asked, "How you doing, hon? Are the pains bad?"

"They're getting close," Bessie uttered.

Violet hurriedly remarked, "Maybe Ona should fetch the doctor before the storm starts."

"Storm, is it really going to be big?" Bessie exclaimed.

Violet related, "Yes we're fixing to have a big snow storm. The snow is coming down hard out there." Violet lifted the curtain back to show Bessie the side of the yard. "See, it's sticking real good. Ona has a good path going out there, so maybe he better fetch the doctor soon. If we send for the doctor now, he can be here before dark."

Bessie took one last breath and looked out the window and said, "Maybe you're right Violet, tell Ona to go for the doctor. I think it's time."

Ona fetched the doctor on horseback and Bessie's brother Frank and sister-in-law Lenah gathered into the house to wait with Violet Letchol. Late that night Bessie gave birth to her first baby.

"It's a girl," the doctor announced as Violet and Lenah helped the doctor clean up the baby and proudly show it off to Ona and the rest of the family. The snowstorm had completely covered the pathway to the house and the doctor had to spend the next two nights at the Beanblossom home before he could make the fifteen mile trip back to Corydon.

Bessie had a hard time relating to motherhood. She lost her mother at the age of three and was raised by her older sister Vie. Vie, being fourteen, made the best of a tough situation but she wasn't your typical mother. Vie took care of the four children and became the only mother Bessie knew. There were so many things Vie taught Bessie, but having a baby was something she had never experienced.

When the storm ended Vie Miller rode four miles down the road to visit her baby sister Bessie. "She sure is a pretty baby," Vie said, "What are you going to name her?"

Bessie related, "We've decided to name her Violet after Violet Letchol. She's been so good to me all these months."

Vie replied, "You two have been close friends all your life. I can see why you would want to name your baby after Violet Letchol."

"Now Vie," Bessie explained, "I also plan to name her after you and Ona. I thought I would call her Violet Theona Beanblossom."

Vie looked puzzled but after a quick review of the name she said, "I guess you will call her Vie for short?"

"That's right, Vie," replied Bessie.

"Well Bessie," Vie related, "you don't have to worry one bit about this baby girl. I'll always be around to help you take good care of her."

Vie was Violet's caregiver. She loved her sister and they were extremely close. When Bessie needed help Vie Miller, her loving sister, was by her side.

Ephesians 1:3-5
Blessed be the God and Father of our Lord Jesus Christ, who chose us in Him before the foundation of the world, that we may be holy and blameless before Him.

Beanblossom place, where Violet was born

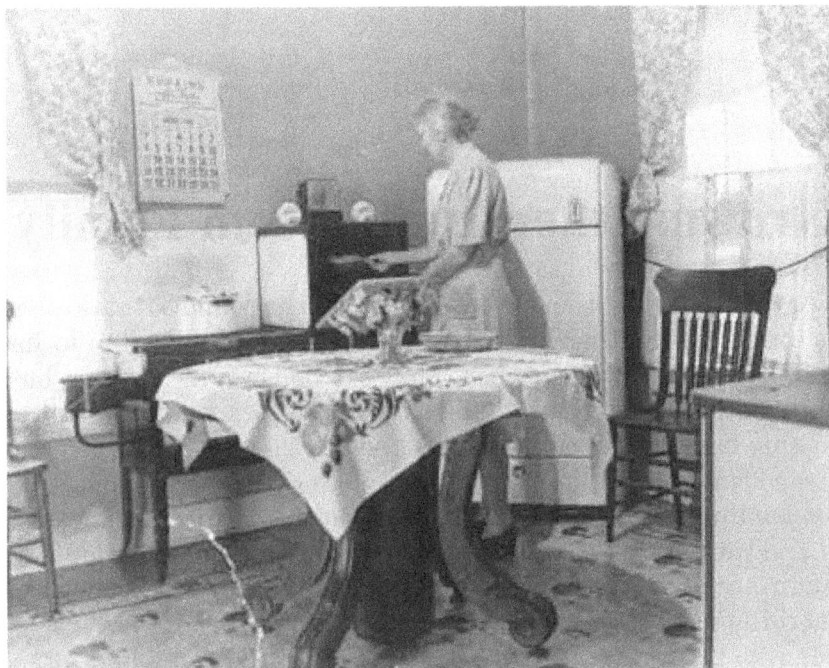

Vie Miller (Bessie's sister)

Vie's house

Growing the Beanblossom Family

A year later Bessie found herself in the same situation. She was expecting another baby in the fall. Bessie didn't plan to have her children so close together, but God had a hand in this birth. From the time she found out that she was expecting, she knew that this baby was special. It was one of those feelings that only a women can experience as she anticipates the baby's birth. The days leading up to her delivery were hard. Morning sickness was evil and preparing each meal was an event that she dreaded. Even though she had given birth to Violet, she knew that there was something different about the way she carried this baby.

It was late November and the leaves on the trees had already turned the customary colors and were making their way to the ground. The farm seemed peaceful except for the sounds of Violet. She was a rambunctious little ten month old packed with dynamite. She was always busy. She was too little to understand that her little world as she knew it was going to come to an end. She was her father's child. She loved being with him and exploring the surroundings of the farm. She was also extremely fond of her aunt, Vie Miller. Somehow she knew she was an only child. She could play each one of them and get what she wanted. Vie adored her niece and enjoyed taking her home to spend the night when Bessie was too tired to take care of her. Violet loved her family and now she was to take on the responsibility of being a big sister. As her story unfolds, you will understand that she took her job seriously until she drew her last breath.

Bessie walked through the house rubbing her abdomen. Looking out the window she could see Ona plowing up the empty corn stalks in the fields. Violet was sleeping on the bed. Naptime would soon be over and she would once again be awake ready to play. Tip toeing pass Violet, Bessie looked at the clock. She was hoping that Ona would soon be bringing in the cows to be milked. It was barely 3:00. The more she walked the more she could feel the pain as it spread through her back down into the tops of her thighs. Looking back across the field she knew she had to face the autumn wind and alert Ona that things were not right. What could be happening to her? She walked over to the calendar and once again calculated the time she had marked off since the doctor had first told her she was expecting. As she bent down to pick up her shoes, she felt a release of blood flow from her body. Knowing that the time was way too soon, she quickly ran out the door and toward the field to flag down Ona. When Ona saw the urgency on her face, he ran to meet her and helped her into the house.

"Bessie, what is going on?"

Bessie began to cry, "I don't know Ona. I think the baby is coming. I am bleeding badly. Help me to the bed and get Lenah."

Ona looked worried. He put on his jacket and replied, "I don't want to leave you here by yourself. Are you sure you'll be okay?"

"Hurry, Ona! I can't wait much longer. Make sure you stop by Violet Letchol's house when you go for the doctor."

Ona said a little prayer as he headed out the door and across the road to tell Bessie's sister-in-law that the baby was coming. Then he rushed down the road to Violet Letchol's house.

Together they all rushed back to the house. Ona wanted to stop one last time before harnessing the horse and heading fifteen miles toward town. Much to his surprise it was too late. Bessie was bleeding and the baby's small head was already out.

Lenah was crying as she took the small baby in her hands and washed off the blood. It was a girl, a very small girl. She was still breathing but everyone standing around the room knew that she was not doing well. Violet Letchol tended to Bessie as she ordered Ona to fetch the doctor.

"Ona, you need to go as fast as you can to get the doctor. It's bad, real bad!"

"Is she going to make it," Lenah asked Ona. "Just fetch the doctor as soon as you can. We'll take good care of her while you're gone."

Ona kissed his wife and left for the barn. The baby let out a small cry.

"Lenah!" cried Bessie, "if I don't make it and the baby lives, will you take her and raise her with your little girl?"

Lenah looked down at Bessie's body now shaking and weak

from labor. "You're going to be fine, Sweetie. We'll raise them together." Lenah knew she was making a promise that she might not be able to keep.

Lenah warmed a brick and placed it in a large shoe box. Then she filled it with cotton batting and tucked the tiny three pound baby into the carefully designed incubator. Bessie had fallen off to sleep and Lenah held her hand as she cried thinking of the future of Bessie and the baby.

"Is she gonna be alright?" yelled Vie as she rushed in through the back door. "Frank told me the baby was already here."

Lenah looked up at Vie. "She's still bleeding bad. I hope the doctor gets here soon. The baby is a girl. She only weighs about three pounds. Look at her she doesn't have any fingernails or eyelashes."

Vie started to cry. "Oh no, please God, take good care of them." Then she ran over to her sister. "Bessie can you hear me?"

Bessie moved her head and tried to open up her eyes. She was so weak that she couldn't speak. "It's okay, Bessie. You just rest and we'll take care of the baby. Everything is going to be just fine."

Ona and the doctor arrived late that night and Violet Letchol helped the doctor take care of Bessie. Together they stopped the bleeding and stayed with her all night. Lenah took care of the baby. The doctor examined the baby and gave some instructions for feeding her with an eye dropper. Lucky for Bessie, her sister-in-law Lenah had given birth just a few months before. She had plenty of milk to nurse the new baby. Lenah took care of the baby just like she was her own. When Bessie regained her strength she and Ona decided on a name. They named her Evelyn Elnora Beanblossom.

Evelyn was very small. This baby needed a lot of attention. Bessie kept her in the shoebox next to the bed where she was warm. Her weight was low and breathing was weak. It was a miracle that she lived. Weeks passed before Bessie could feed the baby by herself. She depended on Vie to help take care of Violet. Violet was full of energy and kept Vie busy. Vie now had another family to take care of. She knew her role in life was to look after her family. She never had any children of her own. She took care of all her nieces and nephews and each one loved her dearly.

Violet loved her baby sister from the day she was born. She

always kept an eye in her direction. Lenah loved her, too. She took care of her like her own baby. Bessie was right, she was special. She was a survivor. Evelyn proved that in many ways. Later when Bessie grew old and needed help, Evelyn became the best caregiver Bessie ever had.

God answered prayer that cold November night. He had a purpose for bringing Evelyn into the world early. Evelyn's birth was a miracle. It was a miracle that they both lived to tell the story. But they lived! Bessie told the story many times. It became a witness that she shared often when she became a preacher's wife. God's surprise! It was more than she had ever expected.

And God smiled that night!

Philippians 4:11-13
I can do all things through Him who strengthens me.

God Gave Us the Fish?

When Violet was old enough to wander around the farm by herself she would spend all day outdoors. She loved being with the animals and watching her father milk cows. One day while Violet was exploring the farm she made friends with Mattie, the little black lady who lived over the hill.

"Hi, my name is Violet," she related, "Do you live around here?"

"I sure do, honey," Mattie replied, "just over the hill there."

Violet asked, "What are you going to do with that pole? Are you going to beat something?"

"No Violet, your family said I could go fishing in your pond. Would you like to go with me?"

"I sure would," Violet exclaimed, "but I ain't got no pole like you do."

"Well now, Miss Violet," Mattie replied, "I guess we better get you a pole and you will also need a pin to make a hook like this. Say, I have an idea, why don't you sit down here and watch me and maybe we can make you a pole later."

"Okay," Violet said.

Looking around Mattie said, "Now where did I put those worms? Oh, here they are."

"I suppose fish like worms?" asked Violet.

"They sure do!" Mattie related. "Now you have to keep quite so you don't scare the fish off."

Whispering in a soft voice Violet continued her conversation.

"Do these fish have names?"

"I don't think so," Mattie whispered.

"Does it hurt the fish real bad when you hook them?"

"I don't rightly know," Mattie responded, "but I do know that the good Lord put those fish in the water for us to eat, and that is just what I am aiming to do." Just as Mattie finished her small talk with Violet she hooked herself a little catfish.

"Wow, Mattie, you did it!" Violet exclaimed. "You caught yourself a real fish. Can I hold it?"

"Are you gonna eat it?"

"Hold on, Violet, you ask too many questions," Mattie said. "Look we will hold him up and take the hook out of his mouth, and then we want to put this here string through his gills so we can carry him home."

Violet watched as Mattie carefully handled the fish. Violet exclaimed, "I love this fishing, Mattie. I want to catch the next one."

All afternoon Mattie and Violet sat on the bank fishing. When Violet returned home, Bessie and Ona were pretty upset with her. "Violet, where have you been?" Ona asked.

"Oh, Daddy, you won't believe it," Violet responded. "I learned how to fish today. I went fishing with Mattie. We caught three fish."

Ona could see the excitement in Violet's eyes. He wanted to swat her in the worst way. As he started to punish Violet he held back his anger and explained the importance of staying close to home. Everyday Violet watched for Mattie to come over the hill to the little pond. She had her safety pin ready and found her a long stick out by the barn. Mattie kept her promise. She came by the house on weekends and took Violet fishing. Soon Violet found that fishing was the love of her life. It was a way to escape her problems. She found herself sitting on the little bank fishing every free minute of the day. Ona saw that Violet enjoyed fishing and when she slipped away from the family, he could count on her being down by the pond sitting there thinking and fishing. When she got lucky and caught a fish, she was happy to share the catch of the day with her family. When Evelyn asked her why she took that poor little fish out of its home, she would explain,

"Evelyn, the good Lord put those fish in there for us to eat and so we should eat them and say thank you."

May God save you from fishing in empty ponds. Do His will and your ponds will be blessed with more fish than you can even store to eat.

Matthew 4:19
    "Come, follow me," Jesus said, and "I will make you fishers of men."

Adventure

Life on the farm was hard. Everything you ate came from the land. Preparing food became a full time job for women living on the farm. The only way to survive was to grow your own crops. They canned food and planned for the winter months when the weather didn't permit fresh food from the garden. Violet learned how to survive from the best. Bessie and Vie worked hard to keep food on the table and clothes on the backs of their family. They often included Violet in their daily chores.

One afternoon while picking dewberries with her mom and aunt, Violet found a large turtle. Carefully sneaking upon what looked like a huge rock sitting in the weeds, Violet screamed out, "Mom, come here I found something."

Looking up from the berry patch, Bessie smiled and remarked. "What in the world did that child find now? I sure hope it isn't a snake. Everywhere I take her she wanders off and looks for adventure."

Violet continued, "Mom, come quick. You won't believe what I just found."

"Okay, Violet, we're coming," yelled Bessie.

Vie and Bessie took off over the hill to find Violet. Sitting right in front of her was the biggest turtle Bessie had ever seen. Bessie turned to her sister and said, "Look, Vie she found herself a turtle."

Violet couldn't stop asking questions. She ran around in circles asking, "Can I keep it, Mom?"

Bessie laughed and replied, "Keep it! Why, many a folk would like to have this turtle to eat."

"I am not much on cooking turtle, Bessie," remarked Vie.

"Maybe one of the other cousins would want to cook it"

Bessie had other plans for the turtle. She quickly replied, "No, Vie! I have an idea. We could take this into town and sell it. I bet we could get money for a big turtle like this."

Violet saw the excitement in her mother's face and shouted, "You mean I found something useful?"

"You sure did, Violet," said Bessie. "We will get Daddy to come up here and pull it home with the sled. Now go gather your berries and let's start for home."

The next day Ona, Violet, Bessie and Vie put the turtle into the back of the wagon and went into town.

Violet leaned up on the counter to watch as the whole family eyed the storekeeper. The old man turned the turtle over and looked at the meat. Watching the reaction of the storekeeper, Violet knew that he was pleased. Turning the animal over he tugged at the legs and said, "Looks like good eating to me. I'll give you three dollars for this turtle miss."

They all jumped for joy alerting the whole store that something wonderful had just taken place. Bessie was eager to gather her money. Before she consulted with her family, she quickly said, "I'll take it!"

Three dollars was a lot of money for 1923. Even though it was a lot of money, the three dollars didn't last long in the hands of the two sisters. Vie had already found some beautiful material that she could use to make the girls some dresses.

"Here, Bessie, buy this material," said Vie. "The girls need clothes, especially Violet. I think I can make her three dresses out of this material,"

"Good thinking, Vie! Maybe some flour and sugar while we're here?"

"Sounds good," said Bessie.

By the time Ona eyed something special to buy, Vie and Bessie had already bought the material, traded their eggs for flour and sugar and were on their way back to the wagon. "Where you going, Ona?" asked Bessie.

"I needed some things from over there," replied Ona, pointing in the direction of the rakes and garden tools.

"Well I hope you have money," replied Vie as she laughingly pushed her way through the store. "Bessie and I are broke."

"That's the fastest money made and spent all in one weekend." laughed Bessie."

"What do you say, Bessie, think we should go berry pickin'

again tomorrow?" laughed Vie.

Ona heard them laughing and turned around and headed toward the wagon. "I guess you girls win this time," said Ona. "Let's go home and make dresses."

Philippians 4:19
My God shall supply all our needs according to his riches in glory by Christ Jesus.

Spring on the Farm

Spring was a wonderful time for gathering food, especially mushrooms.

Violet recalls, the first time she was introduced to mushrooms.

It was a warm spring day and Daddy was driving the buggy over a small creek.

He spotted mushrooms growing in the field. Quickly he stopped the buggy and ran like a rabbit to the unfamiliar objects growing in the field. Then he came back to get me. I first thought he had lost his mind. Then he lifted me down on to the grassy field. He directed me toward several patches of mushrooms.

"You see those trees over there?" Daddy explained, "After a good old April rain you will find beautiful mushrooms."

We walked into the woods and he began to educate me on the art of mushroom hunting.

"Now I want you to look at this one real good," said Daddy. "It's not the kind we find in the grass in front of the barn. These are the only kind of mushrooms you can eat. You must never eat a mushroom before you bring it home for Mom and me to look at." As he gathered the mushrooms he continued to tell me about the wonderful taste. Daddy said, "We call these dry land fish. We'll take these back home and have Mom flour them and fry them up for supper just like we do with the fish you catch."

I soon learned that I loved the taste of mushrooms. Little did I know that someday I too would share this tradition with my children and grandchildren. In Indiana it was a treat to pick and share mushrooms with your friends and family. Daddy was right. It was like having a fish fry. It was a time to celebrate the hunt. Who got the biggest? Who got the most? Where did you get them? Just like keeping your fishing hole a secret, you always kept your mushroom pickin' place a secret. There were always things that most people in small towns didn't need to know. In Harrison County, you didn't give out mushroom gardens. Ha!

Reading my mom's mushroom story reminds me of my relationship with mom and mushrooms.

I can remember that my mom (Violet) always liked taking long trips on lonely country roads in the spring of the year. I didn't realize that she was on a mission to find mushrooms. She would pile us kids in the car on Sundays after church and drive to Indiana. We would look at trees, budding plants and sometimes stop to gather greens called poke. Her true mission was to find mushrooms. If we had known that we were on a mission to find mushrooms, I am sure we would not have settled for a long ride. Exciting things always happened on these mushroom hunts. I remember once following a truck with ears of popcorn stacked in the back. The truck was losing ears of corn as it bumped up and down on the rocky road. Popcorn was everywhere. We would stop and each one of us would take turns getting out of the car to pick up ears of corn. We took the popcorn home and popped it. What a treat! On other mushroom hunts traveling through the country, we brought back baby rabbits, chicks and once even a lamb. The best part of the long ride for me was stopping for ice cream. I hate the country and only choose to be outdoors when I am sitting in the sun reading a book.

Mom never forgot her roots. Just like her mother Bessie, she loved the ability to get her hands dirty and be outside. She loved planting a garden, growing beans, tomatoes and peppers. She canned corn, peaches, and tomatoes. This was a very important ritual. Along with vegetables she loved flowers. Mom planted all kinds of flowers. Once when I was just a small child I was following her in her flower bed as she was setting out rows of different kinds of flowers. The flower bed was muddy and mom was barefooted. Seeing that I was walking behind her, she called out, "Linda, get out of this mud. You are going to step on my flowers."

I replied, "Don't worry mom, I am following in your footprints."

Mom started to cry. I couldn't figure out what I had said to make her so unhappy. I kept those memories in my heart and later realize that following in her footprints carried a large responsibility for mom.

I know for certain that spring was her favorite season of the year. In all of her journaling she was looking forward to the spring. Going fishing and being in the country.

It has taken years for me to realize that each one of us needs a mushroom day. We need a day to take off from work and turn our thoughts toward spring. A new beginning! New growth!

It's a time when everything seems to come to life. I know now that gathering the mushrooms were just a way to reach back and relive the simple days that were free of stress and full of pleasure. Violet had few stress free days. The solitude of a spring day certainly produced the freedom she longed for. For every problem God promises that spring will once again return to chase away the clouds of sorrow.

Thank You, God for the Spring in our days. May we never forget that each day is a gift from You, and may we always give You the glory You deserve.

Matthew 6:8
   Your father knoweth what things ye have need of, before ye ask Him.

School Days in the 1920s

Being free to roam over the farm and spend time with Aunt Vie was such a treat for Violet. She had no idea that time was nearing for her to attend school. This would take her away from all the things she loved doing each day.

When Violet turned six, Bessie took her over to the schoolhouse and told her about school. She tried to make it sound like a wonderful place to spend the day. Violet didn't think much about this new stage in her life, after all, she was too busy in her carefree world to stop and think about leaving the comforts of home.

The summer slipped by quickly. Fall was in the air and children all over the small town of Laconia knew that school was ready to start. Violet was young and clueless. Bessie and Ona reminded her that school was starting and she was now big enough to join her cousins in the little school house down the road. Still she was not aware of what would be expected of her.

The day before school, Bessie took Violet, Evelyn and a neighbor girl to the barn to harness the only horse they owned. Then they hooked the horse up to the buggy and pulled it out in back of the house. Bessie was eight months pregnant. She didn't really feel like going into town, but she knew that Violet needed clothes and school supplies. She gathered up a case of eggs, and a can of cream. They headed into town ten miles away as the girls laughed and exchanged stories of what children do in the little schoolhouse in Dogwood.

It was a good shopping day for the family. Bessie bought material for dresses, shoes for Violet, and even had enough money left over to shop for the new baby.

Each day Bessie had to pack a lunch for Violet to eat at school. Her first lunch was bologna and cheese. This was a treat. Most all of the kids had buckets filled with last night's leftovers wrapped in cheese cloth. They would gather around the well and take turns drinking out of the bucket of water that was lifted from the hole in the ground. It was fun the first few weeks. Recess was the best part.

Then, after a few days locked up in that one room schoolhouse, the excitement wore off and Violet hated school. She cried every day. One day Violet looked across the field, and wishing she were playing with the dogs and cats at home, she failed to see her teacher identify the word "do". When it came time for her to read the sentence on the board, she had no idea what it said. Violet's mind was not focusing on the teacher's comments. She was thinking of projects she was planning to spearhead once she left the confinement of the one room schoolhouse. Playing with her cousins and her sister Evelyn was much more exciting than sitting in school. There had to be some way to get out of this assignment.

"Violet, are you listening to me?" asked the young teacher.

"Oh, yes ma'am!" replied Violet.

"Well Violet," the teacher smugly suggested, "then tell me what this word is."

While the teacher pointed to the word *do*, Violet pronounced the word and failed at every attempt to call it correctly.

Knowing that Violet was not paying attention the teacher scolded her saying, "Look, young lady, you just go stand in the corner until you can pronounce that word correctly."

As Violet stood at attention in the corner, big tears streamed down her face and she wished she were home with her sister Evelyn.

It wasn't long before Violet's contagious personality began to affect the classroom. She was liked by all the kids and made lots of friends. She was smart, and learned the hard way that pleasing the teacher meant that she would have to listen in class and do her work as the teacher requested. She soon loved school. She loved to read and enjoyed participating in class activities. Violet was doing just fine in school until she was distracted by another new addition to her family.

On October 29, 1925, Bessie gave birth to yet another little girl, whom they named Lula Christeen Beanblossom. It was a beautiful fall Saturday and the girls were out of school. Ona sent the children across the field to stay with neighbors as the family gathered in to help Bessie with the birth. The girls stayed within sight of the back door. They knew that Ona would call for them as soon as the baby arrived. Just like before, the baby was born at home with the help of neighbors and relatives.

Violet walked across a small log thinking about the new baby as she questioned Evelyn, "Say, Evelyn, what do you want, a baby brother or a baby sister?"

"I hope it's a sister," said Evelyn as she ran back and forth looking toward the house to see if Ona was coming to share the news.

"It sure does take a long time to have a baby." said Evelyn as Violet took off her shoes and waded in the creek picking up small rocks along the way.

"I am going to be the first to hold her," said Violet. "I am the oldest and I should be the first to hold the baby." As she bragged she glanced at the house one last time and saw her father standing at the gate. Violet pushed Evelyn in the direction of her father as she screamed, "Oh look, Evelyn. The baby is here. Come on, let's go see the baby."

Ona was motioning for the girls to come up to the house. They ran together toward their father. He quickly took them both in his arms and told them they had a baby sister. The other children followed them. They all rushed into the bedroom to see the new baby.

"She looks like a little possum," said one neighbor boy who was eyeing her small hand.

"She looks like my little sister," said Evelyn as she watched Violet pick her up and hold her carefully in her arms.

"Mom, do you think I should stay home from school on Monday and help you with the baby?" asked Violet.

Bessie laughed as she assured Violet that she would be fine on her own. The next day Ona went into town and bought bologna, cheese and crackers for the family to eat while Bessie rested in bed. This was a special treat for the kids. Friends and neighbors also brought in food for the family and all the excitement made it hard for Violet to return to school on Monday.

Bessie had an easy birth this time. She was able to give orders from her bed and the first order was that Violet must return to school. Making this quite clear, Bessie suggested that she needed to return to school to tell her classmates about the new baby.

Taking this into consideration, Violet started to plan how she would capture the attention of the whole class. She liked to tell stories and this would make a wonderful story that no one would be able to top. Violet couldn't wait for school to start. She had a secret and it needed to be shared. Sharing stories about her sisters gave her plenty of things to share at show and tell, until Evelyn showed up at school and told her own version of home stories.

The next year Evelyn got to walk to school with Violet. Evelyn was shy, and attached to her Mom. She was very different from her sister Violet. She hated school and didn't really like playing games with the others.

In the winter when the pond on the farm was frozen, the teacher would take all the class over behind the Beanblossom house and let them skate at playtime. They didn't have ice skates. Without any fear of falling through the ice, each child pretended to skate using only the shoes they had on their feet. Most had holes and were stuffed with cardboard. Recess was thirty minutes in the morning and thirty minutes in the afternoon.

The wind was cold and the younger kids would be freezing, especially if they didn't have on long underwear.

The older children would be caregivers for the younger children. Often they would give up hats and coats to keep the little children warm. The school had grades one through twelve. There was a big pot belly stove in the middle of the room and a bench for reciting lessons in the front of the room.

Each grade would take turns going to the bench to learn their lessons from the teacher. Children not reciting or sitting on the bench were sitting in small desk working on lessons assigned by the teacher on the blackboard. The school was never full. Most children dropped out after grade school to work on the farm.

Farming was everyone's life. Most families had large families so the children could help on the farm.

Violet relates,

"We got up early to do our chores. Ran home to do chores after school and went to bed early right after supper. We were lucky that we were not boys. I am sure we would have not finished school."

The girls didn't complain about their lack of possessions. They were very poor, but so was everyone else in Dogwood.

Matthew 6:20-21
  "But lay up for yourselves treasures in heaven where neither moth nor rust doth corrupt, and where thieves do not break through nor steal. For where your treasure is, there your heart will be also."

Bessie and her daughters

Food on the Farm

The children enjoyed the farm, their neighbors, and cousins.

Violet writes,
I remember when we killed our hogs to eat and sell. Sometimes we killed four or five at a time. The men got up early and heated water in the big black iron kettles. After they killed the hogs, they would put them on a sled to bring them close to the house. We heated hot water in a barrel to dip the hogs in so we could scrape the hair from the bodies. It didn't take them long to cut them up and put them in the smoke house where we cured the meat. The tenderloins would be so good you didn't have to smoke them just to eat them. The rest was smoked and we had good country ham in about six weeks. This also gave us bacon and sausage. We used the fat for lard to cook with and to make lye soap. There was lots of work to be done on the farm. Water was a simple chore that Evelyn and I always did together.

One evening, knowing it was time for supper, Violet yelled, "Come on Evelyn, let's go across the street and get water for supper."

Picking up their pails they made the journey to the well. They pulled the rope up and filled their buckets from the big bucket at the end of the rope.

"You know, Evelyn," remarked Violet, "this reminds me of the woman at the well in the Bible. I wonder if she had to pull up her water like we do."

As Evelyn leaned down to look at the big hole, Violet grabbed her. "Don't get too close to that well," Violet cautioned, "I am always afraid that one of us will get lost down there and never make it home. Here, let me help you pour the water into the pail.

We'll make it across the street and then stop for a rest on the big rock so we can make it the rest of the way home."

They always had chores to do from morning till night. Violet helped milk cows and Evelyn helped bring in fire wood. All of the girls took on the job of cooking and cleaning right alongside of Bessie.

In the summer it was the women who tended the garden and canned food to store in the cellar for the winter.

Violet writes,

My mother Bessie could always find us food to eat. She would cook cornbread and mix it with milk and we thought this was the best we ever had. When she could get sugar, she loved to make us candy.

The Beanblossom girls lived about four miles from their Grandpa Eckert and Aunt Vie. They would spend the weekends with Vie. Vie was always cooking and making good things to eat. She was very creative considering what she had to work with. In the winter men would cut thick slabs of ice from the pond and put them in the cellar with lots and lots of saw dust. This helped to keep things cold. In the summer Vie would make ice cream. What a thrill to have company over to sit on the porch and eat fresh ice cream. Making the ice cream was entertainment for the family. They all took turns spinning the cream until it was nice and frozen, ready to eat. Aunt Vie also made good taffy. Making good taffy was important. Taffy pulls were social events for the young people. It was a chance to meet new boys and girls in the community. Having Aunt Vie make taffy was an advantage for Violet. Whoever had the taffy could be the one to invite others to the party. Violet liked parties and it was easy to convince Aunt Vie to make her famous taffy. Trading house cleaning for taffy was a kind gesture that Aunt Vie always welcomed.

Violet recalls,

I can remember Aunt Vie would keep her house so nice and clean. She had lots of nice things all organized and neatly placed around the room. In the spring she would take up the woven rug and hang it on the line to air out while she dusted it by beating it with a huge stick. Then she would sweep up the old sawdust that acted like a pad under the rug and replace it with new. Any tears in the rug would be mended and the rug would be placed back on the old wooden planks good as new.

As the girls grew older they had more chores to do to keep the family alive. They would gather eggs and take them to a store across the street to trade for food. The family was grateful for any food they had. Some families did not have screens on the windows and the doors. Animals were close by and the flies were plentiful. The girls didn't sleep late in the mornings and they didn't nap in the afternoons. They would always be doing some kind of chores to help with food and clothing. It was very hot in the afternoons.

Violet remembers,

When men came to our farms in the summer to help with the thrashing of our wheat and oats, my mother was sure that everyone knew how important it was that we took care of the men who came to help out.

"Come on, kids, let's get moving," called Bessie, as she moved through the kitchen, checking the contents of the little cabinet near the window. "The thrashing men will be here tomorrow and we all have to pitch in and help get meals ready. They'll be plenty hungry when they come out of the fields for lunch and supper. Violet, you and Evelyn pick some berries, 'cause I am going to bake a few pies. Some of the others are bringing their corn, beans and tomatoes. Vie and I will fry up a big chicken and country ham from the cold cellar. It might take the men all week to finish everyone's fields. We all have to work together to make it through the summer."

"Don't look so ungrateful, Violet," Bessie would scold.

Violet replied, "I guess this means that all the kids have to stand over the table and fan the food to keep the flies away?"

Bessie nodded, "You're right, Violet, so round up some of your cousins and find the biggest branches you can find. We'll need all of you to shoo the flies away. Remember, the men eat first, and then you kids can eat what's left."

(After lunch, a tablecloth was spread over the food and everyone took their place back at the table for supper. There was no type of refrigeration in between meals. Food was warmed over and no one seemed to get food poisoning.)

Salt was a very important preservative on the farm. The knowhow to use it, made eating both savory and safer. Jesus calls Christians the salt of the earth. We should be the "Salt" that sprinkles the true love, joy and hope on this confused and corrupted world.

Matthew 5:13
"*Ye are the salt of the earth, but if the salt have lost his savor, wherewith shall it be salted?*"

Violet and Sisters

The Farm House

Violet writes,

I loved the farm. I can remember the old house and everything that happened there both good and bad. My mother was always there to encourage us girls to do our chores and get our lessons. Our father worked hard to put food on the table, but he also taught us the Bible and the importance of prayer.

"Come on, girls, it's time to get your lessons," called Bessie as she cleaned the light globes and lit the lamps filled with oil. "Your daddy will be home soon and then we'll have to go straight to bed."

"I can recite this whole page of poetry," Violet would call out. "Want to hear me?

"No!" called Evelyn, "Just because you like school doesn't mean you have to always show off and teach us everything you learn. Besides, I have my own lessons to get."

Bessie interrupted, "Now girls, finish your work and I am going to get some firewood for the night and when I return I want to see both of you ready for bed."

As Bessie draped herself with a ragged coat and scarf, Evelyn and Violet studied next to the dimly lit lamp. Most evenings they would write out their lessons by the light of the fireplace along with the light of the lamp. As usual, it was freezing in the little house in the winter. The girls dressed in warm wool nightshirts, long underwear with a flap in the back and climbed into bed. When Bessie returned with the wood she put covers over the girls and heated the heavy iron. Then she wrapped it in a small blanket to warm the bottom of the bed. This would keep the kids feet warm until they could fall asleep. There were so many covers on the bed that the girls could hardly turn over. Baby Teen slept with Bessie and Ona to stay warm. She moved to the older girl's bed when she was old enough to sleep with them without being squashed in the middle. Ona would always kneel by the side of the old bed and say prayers with the family. The house was cold in the winter and very hot in the summer. Despite the temperature of the season, the love of a Christian father warmed the hearts of each child. Ona never missed a night reading the Bible and praying for each girl. His little family was the most important thing in Ona's life. No lights, no bathtub, and no indoor plumbing, but they were happy and didn't realize that they were very poor.

In those days no one in town had indoor plumbing. The toilets were holes in wooden planks that you sat on in little buildings called *outhouses*. If you needed paper you used a page out of the Sears catalogue or maybe a few big leaves. There were no bathtubs to take baths. Once a week a fire would be built in the fireplace to warm the house and then a wash tub was filled with warm water for a bath. Each one of the family members took turns bathing. They scrubbed with lye soap that was made from ashes and lard. Making soap was another project performed by family members. This type of soap was also used for washing clothes. In between baths, water was warmed and placed in a small water basin. This allowed the family to wash hands and faces before getting dressed in the morning and again before bed.

Washing clothes was a whole day's work. All the clothes were scrubbed on a scrub board or wash board. This was a small wrinkled metal board that could be placed in a tub. Lye soap was used to lather the clothes and scrub out the dirt. It was a tiring job for the lady of the house. When it was warm outside, Bessie would go down by the stream behind the house and do the wash. Bessie would then take the clothes home where they were hung out to dry. Heavy irons were heated on the fireplace and used to press wrinkles from cotton clothing. The iron was very heavy. It had to be heated many times to get all the wrinkles out.

The girls' underwear was made out of cloth feed sacks. All the girls in town had the same kind of underwear. Sometimes the pattern of the feed sacks would change. This was a happy day for little girls all over town. Violet and Evelyn would watch for the wagon to pull up on Saturdays to see what the feed sacks looked like. This would let them know what color their new underwear was going to be. There was one pattern for making underwear, and

Bessie and Vie would make underwear to fit each girl. Then cutting the pattern bigger, they would make underwear for themselves.

When each girl started her menstrual period, she would have to use special torn up rags that would be washed out and be reused just for that purpose. This was a challenge for any young girl. They had to attend school and go to the outhouse to use the bathroom. Then they had to carry home dirty rags to be washed out and dried for another use.

Diapers were not washed if they were just wet by the baby. Women would just hang the diapers on the line to dry and you could smell the urine in the air as you passed them in the yard. When the diaper was dry, it was placed back on the baby just like new. Baby clothes were made mostly by the older women and passed down to cousins and neighbors who were expecting babies.

In her diary Violet writes,

As little girls we enjoyed pretending and playing games with other families and friends. Sundays after church we would go down to the creek and swing on the grapevine. We had lots of places to make playhouses. Our special recipe was mud pie sometimes filled with rocks. Our dolls were made out of corn silks. Some had red hair and some had white hair. We loved our dolls just like they were real babies. Like all other little girls, we played mommies and daddies, taking our dolls to church and to town.

We didn't have many toys, but I will never forget the day Evelyn and I were given a wonderful surprise by our grandfather Beanblossom.

"Hurry up, Evelyn," Violet exclaimed, "Grandpa is calling for us to come outside to help him bring in the corn."

"Why are you so excited about a load of corn, Violet?" asked Evelyn.

Evelyn proclaimed, "He just wants to put us to work."

"No," Violet protested, "he said he has a surprise for us. Come on, I love surprises."

As the two girls unloaded the corn, there was a little red wagon under the corn stalks.

"Oh, Evelyn," Violet said excitedly. "Have you ever seen

anything so beautiful in your entire life?"

"Is it ours, Grandpa?" asked Evelyn.

"You bet!" he said.

Both of us girls screamed and carried on as if we had been given a brand new car. Immediately we took turns pulling each other up and down the hill. Every night we would take the red wagon and fetch wood for the stove. We always went together to keep each other company. Staying together became important to Violet.

Animals took the place of toys. Cows, pigs, chickens and a pet dog named Collie were their animal playmates.

Collie the dog was a distraction for the girls. He kept them from thinking about chores, school and being poor. Collie was their first real pet. He roamed the hills of southern Indiana and could always find his way home.

Violet writes,

In the late afternoons Evelyn and I would look for Collie as an excuse to see what our cousins were doing down the road. I can still feel the evening breeze following us down the dusty rock road. We called for our dog, but we were secretly wondering what our cousins were having for supper. There was always someone sitting on the porch at my uncle's house. We would stop to talk or play games. I loved going there because my aunt was a wonderful cook. If we were lucky, we were invited to snack on something good that she had just taken out of the oven. Evelyn and I were warmly welcomed and mostly expected because we had pulled this stunt more than once to get away from home and visit with our cousins. One afternoon when we went to visit our cousins, Lester and Cora, Lester was trying to catch a piglet. Catching piglets was a game to show all the other kids how brave you were. Lester was a show off. He delighted in entertaining us with this risky little game. I remember this one day the old sow raised up her head and ran for all of the children walking around the pig pen. Our dog, Collie, came to the rescue. He stood between the piglet and Lester long enough for all of us to reach the fence and tumble over.

On Sundays Collie would sit at the top of the hill until she could see our car come home from church. Then she would jump on the sideboard of the car and ride the rest the way home with the family. He was a real working farm dog. In the evenings it was a beautiful sight to say "Collie, go bring the cows down in the fields." He would run up the hill and over the fields to fetch all the cows. He would use his special technique of biting the back of the cow's hoofs making them run toward home and into the barn. Each cow knew its own stall. They remained still in the stall until we milked then and bedded them down with straw. Mom, dad and I milked every night before supper. I didn't mind the milking too much. I had a favorite cow named Blackie. She was always willing to give me her best.

Jesus loved animals and provided them for food as well as pleasure. He knew that the family depended on the farm animals. I find it awesome that he also provided protection and help for the family with Collie the dog.

The love of God for people and animals was passed on through Noah's blind faith. Lord, give us the faith of Noah.

Genesis 9:16-17
"And the bow shall be in the clouds. I will look upon it, that I may remember the everlasting covenant between God and every living creature of all flesh that is upon the earth." And God said to Noah, "This is the token of covenant, which I have established."

Growing Up Too Soon

Violet loved her family; however, her life began to change at a very young age. Ona's father and brother came to live with the family. Ona and his father went together and bought a 114 acre farm near Dogwood, Indiana closer to Vie and Bessie's father, Chris. Ona wasn't much of a farmer. Ona's father was wonderful to the family. For seven years they struggled to grow crops and keep food on the table. Ona needed the extra hand and advice that his father gave him. He wanted to be a good farmer. Growing more crops would allow him to make more money for his family. His brother wasn't much help. He was mentally ill and could only do little chores assigned to him. Ona didn't realize that having extra family members to take care of was more work for Bessie. He was focusing on farming. He now had more land and needed another farm hand. Ona also didn't realize that his little girls were silently suffering.

Violet writes in her story,

Grandpa, my mother's dad, always wanted to follow me to the woodshed. He would make me pull down my drawers and tell me to make it wink at him. I was so afraid when this first happened. I couldn't tell daddy. I really didn't know what he was trying to do. I just knew that it wasn't right to show your underwear to men. Little did I know that my grandfather was trying to rape me. I remember daddy would get busy on the farm, and he would have our other grandfather pick us up from school. He would ride on the old white horse and have me ride in front of him. He would then place his hands in between my legs. It hurt me badly when he rubbed his rough raw hands against my skin. He would usually meet us in the wheat field at the bottom of the hill and follow us the rest the way home. This is where he and my uncle would abuse us. My uncle, who was my father's brother, also abused us. He was kicked in the head by a horse when he was a child and he was mentally disabled. He tried to make the sexual abuse a game. Maybe in his mind it was, but it would linger in our heads and hearts forever.

One day I had had enough! I saw my grandfather take my little sister Evelyn to the barn and I ran as fast as I could to tell my mother.

I screamed, "Mom, grandpa is taking Evelyn up to the barn to make her take her pants off and make it wink at him."

Boy, my mother was mad. She headed right to the field to get my father and we soon left the farm. I later found out that my grandfather had raped all my girl cousins who lived down the road. Nothing was said or done about anything back then. We just knew to stay away from our abusers. A lot of things happened like this in the schoolyards and corncribs of little towns. No one ever got caught or punished. Who knows, my mother may have been raped by her own father. She never told us anything about her life or her relationship with her father. What a shame. He was sexually abusing all of his granddaughters who lived close by.

Ona was furious! He ordered his father-in-law away from his house and sent his brother away. He was praying about going into the ministry and now he felt that God was trying to tell him something. Daily he prayed for answers.

It was here in Violet and Evelyn's life that they became "victims." Their life would never be the same. They were overpowered by someone they trusted. Their abuse was physical and brought on fears and insecurities. Even though the damage had been done, God provided a way out. He gave Ona hope of a new life that would take the family away from the farm.

There are so many children in the world today that are being abused both physically and mentally. It is in Jesus that we learn to overcome our suffering and look to God for protection. Violet learned to trust God, but her trust in others was never restored.

She never learned to respect or love herself. She was deeply wounded and fearful of relationships that required unconditional love.

Instead of showing weakness, it was her character to pretend that things were normal. She became a wonderful actor. She believed that you must be strong in all situations. She was always looking for approval from others to feel good about herself. She loved to entertain and party at her house. Bringing groups of people together gave her false belief that she was certain others loved her and felt her important. Often people took advantage of Violet and her generosity.

1 Corinthians 4:5
He will bring to light what is hidden in darkness and expose the motives of men's hearts.

Kids Play

Violet was still adventurous as a teenager. She was willing to try new things especially when her cousin Lester dared her.

Violet writes,

One evening as my parents headed to church, I remember hitching our horse to a sled. It was spring, and of course Lester and Cora were in on the fun. We all climbed aboard letting the horse pull us through the grass. Of course we only did this when we were left alone. Daddy would have had my hide if I pulled a stunt like this with him around. Anyway, my cousin Lester, who was one year older than I am, knew how to put the harness on the hitch and we pulled the sled around giving all the kids rides. Wow that was the most fun we had had in months. Little did we realize that the sled left marks in the grass, and sure enough, my dad found out about our little game. I was punished and so was Lester. Mom and dad believed in spanking and once you were spanked you didn't repeat the offence.

When the teen years hit, our games changed. We played running games like fox and the hound, hide and seek, spin the bottle and some others that were so exciting that I forgot what they were.

We had no TV only a radio and it wasn't used a lot. We were not allowed to go to the show or play cards. These activities were sinful, so we made our own entertainment mostly with family and church friends. This is where the taffy pull came in handy. We invited kids over to sit on our porch to pull taffy or make ice cream. When we got tired of that we would catch lighting bugs and scare each other in the dark. Wow, what fun!

We looked forward to spring and summer so we could go barefooted. I remember mom ordering us tennis shoes from the Sears and Roebuck catalog. Mine were blue and Evelyn's were yellow. We were so proud of the shoes that we couldn't wait to show them to Daddy. We put them on and ran all the way down to the field where Daddy was plowing to show him our new shoes. After everyone in the neighborhood saw our shoes, we took them off and went barefooted. We had never had new shoes so sporty and stylish. It only made sense to us that we take them off so they would not get dirty on the bottom.

It was wonderful that Violet had a Christian family and grew up in the church. Most teens that are abused turn to drugs, sex or alcohol. I am sure she was blaming herself for the things that happened in her life. Being the oldest was also a big responsibility. She took on the role of caregiver to both of her sisters. She protected them and went to extremes to nurture and boss them around. Her personality grew as she participated in school activities and made new friends. She looked for courage to step out of her comfort zone and try new things. In her teen years she learned that she could be a leader.

Galatians 6:2,5
   Bear one another's burdens, and thus fulfill the law of Christ. For each one shall bear his own load.

Ona Surrenders to the Call

The Beanblossom family never missed a Sunday going to church.

Violet remembers,

I can't remember a time in my childhood that our family was absent from church on Sunday morning. We attended the EUB Church, which was located at Smith's Camp Ground in Laconia Indiana. The church was something special. My grandpa Eckart and his brother built it back in the early 1800s. It has a small cemetery in the side yard where most of my relatives are buried. In 1929 I lost both of my grandfathers. We had a service for each of them in that little church and they were buried outside with the rest of the family that went on to meet Jesus in heaven. Even though it brought about some sad times for our family, it also gave us some good memories. I can remember having picnics, ice cream socials, and pie suppers at that little white church. Most of my entertainment was centered around church activities.

The summers went fast for Violet. It was lots of hard work living on the farm but being outside was just what she enjoyed. Ona still wasn't much of a farmer. He had worked hard on the 114 acre farm. Family and friends often jumped in to help him bring in crops. Even though he worked from sun up to sun down for seven years, things got bad: no money and little food. The family had to move into New Albany so Ona could work a steady job in the lumber mill. After a year in New Albany, Ona was called into the ministry. He knew his love of the Lord needed to be shared with others. He had been fighting the call for a long time. Ona would pray in the fields as he worked. He was saved and gave Jesus his life one day under a tree as he worked and prayed daily. He knew that he loved the Lord and he knew that he was running from the will of God. He told Bessie that he needed to take up his cross and follow Jesus. Bessie was worried, but she knew that Ona was under conviction to preach the word. She knew her husband's heart. Prayerfully Bessie packed up the girls, left her family in Harrison County and followed her husband. He was assigned a church in Edwardsville, Indiana. Little did Violet realize that this was the start of a long tour of little churches in small towns.

Communication in the country was usually at church or visiting on Sundays with neighbors. This was also true in the little town of Edwardsville. Everything centered on church. Violet made lots of new friends but she missed her cousins and family in Laconia. It helped to know that she could still communicate with them by phone. A telephone, hung on the wall in the new house. You rang it by turning a crank.

Violet writes,

Our phone number was one long turn and two short turns. There were ten families on our line. The line was often busy and most of them like to eavesdrop. We had to be very careful what we said. Mom would make sure that we said the right thing and not offend any of our neighbors. Being the preacher's wife she was always aware that people would talk if given any kind of misinformation. The first telephone in Harrison Co. was in 1917. We had a telephone when I was born. It doesn't make sense. No washer, toilet or lights but we had a telephone. It was a gift from God!

Christ is worthy of our love and obedience. Ona heard the call to preach the gospel and became obedient to do God's will. At the expense of everything else, Ona responded to God and became a willing servant.

Psalm 73:25-28

Whom have I in heaven but thee? And besides Thee, I desire nothing on earth. But as for me, the nearness of God is my good. I have made the Lord God my refuge, that I may tell of all Thy works.

The Vacation

Violet writes,

We only took one vacation that I can remember.

Ona ran in the house calling out to Bessie.

"Hey, Bessie, call the girls and come outside." Bessie knew that Daddy was excited about something so she did what she was asked and summons us kids to the front of the house.

"Violet, Evelyn, Teen, come quick. Dad has a surprise for us."

The word surprise always perked up the girls ears so it didn't take much to move their behinds down to the front door and notice a Motel T car sitting right in front of the house.

"Is this ours?" asked Teen.

"It's ours," said Daddy, as he took turns placing us all in the car to take a ride around the farmland.

New Car and Vacation

It was the most excitement that the little Beanblossom girls had had in a long time. That summer they loaded up the old Model T Ford and ventured out to see Ona's sister in Champaign, Illinois. Getting ready for a trip in those days was very exhausting. Bessie washed all the family's clothes on a washboard. Then she dried and folded each piece so they would fit in the small, borrowed suitcase. Little Teen was watching closely, and when no one was watching she pulled the tub of water over on her foot and broke her toe.

Evelyn and Violet wanted to break her neck. They thought for sure that their trip was canceled, but to their surprise Bessie didn't get mad. She cleaned up the mess and bandaged Teen's toe. She rewashed the wet clothes in the tub and assured the girls that everything would be just fine. The next day the family headed west.

Violet writes,

We visited all of my dad's sisters and bounced all over the road. We could see the lanterns glowing on other cars as we traveled down dirt roads. The trip seemed to take forever. Can you imagine traveling in a Model T Ford without air conditioning? It was hot and the dust on the roads stuck to your sweaty body. We would sing songs and take short naps to pass the time away. We were so packed into that car. It was hard to move much less breathe. It was the first time the family had ever been to a big town.

We saw people living differently than we had experienced. Our cousins were using toothbrushes and toothpaste. It was sure different than baking soda and lemon on a washcloth. My aunt owned a restaurant and a small grocery store. They had so many nice things that we had never seen. Fine homes, washing machines, soap from the store and nice clothes. Life was easier for them compared to our little life on the farm.

Our growth toward spirituality is a journey. God reveals new and interesting things for us to explore along the way. It's up to us to look, listen and learn all He wants us to know to complete the journey.

Father, help us to stay focused on you as we continue our daily journey to do your will.

Another Year and a New Home

Violet writes,

My dad was a very good minister. At the end of the year, the conference of the United Brethren Church reassigned ministers to new churches. Dad sold all our farm animals except a cow, and we headed to Montgomery, Indiana to pastor a new church. This is where I started a new school. I was in the eighth grade at this new school. I can remember being sad to leave my cousins and friends who lived in Dogwood. We would go home from church with members to eat lunch on Sundays and most of the time stay until church started that night. Many times we fell asleep on church pews while my father preached. Once I recall eating at a member's house that wasn't very clean. We were invited to lunch, and with little or no food at home you didn't pick and choose whom you ate lunch with. We left church and drove over to this little house to eat Sunday dinner. While passing the food around the table, Evelyn and I spotted worms in the macaroni and cheese. We all punched each other and didn't eat any of it. My baby sister Teen took a big old helping and ate all of it. We couldn't get to her before she ate every single bite. Mom, Evelyn and I giggled all through lunch. Dad knew our secret but acted like nothing was wrong. As soon as we could grab Teen away from the table, we shared our little secret. It didn't kill her, but she was so upset when we confessed what we saw that she tried to throw up. Mom announced jokingly, "From now on, girls, always look the food over before you eat. Some of these people may not like the way Daddy preaches.

Galatians 6:9

Let us not be weary in well doing; for in due season we shall reap, if we faint not.

Another School in a New Town

I was sick a lot when I was in school. Dad and I got small pox. The health department came out to our house and quarantined us for twenty one days. People everywhere were dying from this disease. It was a miracle that we lived. A neighbor would get our groceries, put them by a tree down the lane and mom would walk down and pick them up. I also got diphtheria. I was sickly until I had my tonsils out at the age of twelve. Even with ill health, I was still a good student. I loved school.

In 1933, we moved again to Jasonville Indiana. Moving to new schools wasn't fun, especially with a name like Beanblossom. Everyone always made fun of your name and teased you because you were the minister's daughter. I learned to like Jasonville after I met my first boyfriend. His name was Clifford Snyder. I finished the second year of high school and made lots of friends before we had to move again. I played girls basketball. We wore one-piece bottoms that looked like bloomers. My dad had a fit! He didn't like me playing in those evil shorts. He didn't come to any of my games so I didn't talk about it anymore and went ahead and played ball. I played forward on the team and he didn't try to stop me. Ha! I was lucky that none of the church members complained about my outfit. That wasn't the only secret that I kept from him that year. I was in the school play and choir. I had to dance with my girl friend, which was also a preacher's daughter. We made a vow not to tell our parents about the dancing. Mom and dad didn't come to the play and didn't find out about the dance. We had a big crowd there and I was sure someone would tell my parents. I got lucky two times. I loved being a part of the school activities. I only wish my sisters could have shared my luck. Poor Teen couldn't be cheerleader because her skirt was too short. She wanted to wear lipstick like all the other girls, so she wet red crepe paper and put it on her lips to give her color. Being the minister's daughter was a curse as well as a blessing.

We lived in Jasonville during the great depression and it was really bad. Dad didn't get enough money for us to half live on. When they would have board meetings at the church, us girls would listen outside the door to see how much money they were going to give the preacher. We also knew who voted for and against the giving of the money. We would run back and share this information with mom. I don't think Daddy would have approved of our sneaking around but Mom always listened and was never surprised with the information we gathered. Because of the depression, Daddy had to take two churches so we could have more money. Still we ate what was given to us and sometimes went to bed hungry. The depression hit us hard!

Even though times were hard, Ona and Bessie did not give up. What a great inspiration for their children and grandchildren. They had the faith that God was going to take care of them, and He did.

1 Peter 1:7
    These trials are only to test your faith to see whether or not it is strong and pure. It is being tested as fire tests gold.

A New Year and a New Church

When the conference met in the spring, Daddy was moved yet to another church. This time we moved to Lewis, Indiana. This was a little town but it had a high school and I got to ride on a school bus. The school's name was Blackhawk High School. Things were looking up. I attended my junior and part of my senior year at Blackhawk. I was in the school play of Arsenic and Old Lace *in my junior year and I was also cast to be in the senior play. I can't remember the play but I am sure I had a good time. Ha! There wasn't but seventeen kids in my senior class. I loved school and made good grades. My sister Evelyn was only a freshman, but one of our senior boys fell in love with her. He would write her love notes. I would always tease her by reading her letters out loud.*

"To Evelyn Elnora, I can't wait to see you at school tomorrow."

"Oh stop it, Violet, and give me my letters back," Evelyn said as she reached for the paper in Violet's hands.

"Evelyn's got a boyfriend." continued Violet in a sing song voice.

"You're just jealous that he doesn't like you," replied Evelyn.

"Jealous! Why, Evelyn, I could have any boy in the school if I wanted. I just don't think any of them are my type."

Looking at Violet with a smile, Evelyn replied, "Violet! What is your type?"

Violet lingered on the question and then replied, "Well, I'll let you know when they come along. Meanwhile you better hide those love letters from Mom and Dad. Evelyn, I really did read some of those letters and they ARE love notes."

"You have your nerve reading my letters!" said Evelyn. "Besides I don't really like him. He's much too old for me. So there!"

Violet confirmed that Evelyn should have a boyfriend. "He's seventeen and I admit, he is tall and very good looking. I think you should like him back. Your secret is safe with me."

Evelyn gave it some thought and replied, "Well, maybe I will if you promise not to tell."

"I promise," said Violet.

Through the years they kept a lot of secrets from their family. Remembering the last year of school, Violet writes,

> In the middle of the year once again we were moved to start a church in a little town called Coal City. It was there that I finally made it out of high school. I made good grades, but I don't know how with all the moving around. I graduated top in my class. My dad gave our baccalaureate address at the school. I wanted to go to college and be a teacher. My dad spoke to a man who came from Indianapolis College to visit me at my home. Dad would get a discount because of my grades and being a minister's daughter. However, we still didn't have enough money to afford college. I was very disappointed that I would never be able to attend college. I loved to learn. I think I would have been an excellent teacher.

God had a plan for Violet. She continued to teach his word and do his work until the day she died.

Matthew 11:1

> After Jesus had finished instructing his twelve disciples, He went on from there to teach and preach in the towns of Galilee.

Violet's Senior Picture 1935-36

Violet's Love Story

In 1936, my life took a big turn. There wasn't much to do after I graduated from school. Work was hard to find in a small town and I was very unhappy living at home with my strict preacher dad. I remember the last day of school I came home, put my books on the table and said, "Mom, I am free, white, and out of school." My mother looked at me and cried. Somehow I know in her heart that she knew that I would find a difficult world outside of our protected home. I was ready to move on with my life.

That summer, I remember going with dad back to Dogwood to sell our corn that was raised on the farmland that we still owned. The school there was having a pie supper. I didn't want to miss this big event. Each girl would bake a pie and pack it in a box with her name on it. Then the pie would be auctioned off for a boy to buy. The boy who bought the pie had to eat with the girl that made the pie. I met my future husband at that pie supper. His name was Ora Stapleton. He drove a 1934 Ford Roadster that had a top he could turn down.

My cousin, Lester Eckart, and his girlfriend Ann introduced him to me. I spent the night at my aunt's house and he came by and took me for a ride in his car the next day. I can still see him coming down that country road and around the pond with the top down and the rumble seat up. Out of all the crowd of girls that he could have gone out with, he picked me.

We wrote to each other every week. Once a month he would come to see me at Coal City, Indiana where, I was living with my parents. Ora lived in Louisville with his sister. I was miserable during the week. My heart would throb when he came down the road on weekends to take me out. I remember my first real big date with him. He picked up a couple who were his friends, and we all rode down to Laconia. It was not a big deal, but I remember that we went out for cokes. I spent the night with my aunt and went to Smiths Camp Grounds to church. That Sunday night he drove me back to Coal City and he drove back to Louisville, Kentucky where he lived with his sister.

Ora's parents died when he was eleven years old. Their names were Cora and Guy Stapleton. He had a twin brother named Ira. There were eight brothers and sisters in the family. The boys were tossed from sister to sister. Their mother was a schoolteacher. She died at the age of forty-eight and the father died the same year. It was tough on all the kids, especially on the twins. They had no rules and no discipline. They had no sense of right and wrong like others from a two parent Christian home. I learned the hard way that no home is complete without God. I was fortunate that I had Christian parents and I hope that my children will raise their children in Christian homes. Please make sure children are taken to church and learn about God's plan of salvation. Maybe someday we can all be together in heaven.

I know things would have been different if Ora's parents were living. Ora and Ira went to work in Louisville at Brown and Williams Tobacco Company. They were only seventeen years old. Their Uncle Clyde Stapleton was a policeman and had lots of money and clout with the factory. He lied and said they were eighteen. They made good money, and in one year, they both had new cars. Money and cars were enough to turn any girl's head.

In the summer I would stay with my aunt who still lived in Laconia where Ora's family lived. I would take off and spend time in Laconia so I could see Ora. We always had a good time together, spending time with his family. One weekend he came to Coal City and asked me to marry him. I was so excited I immediately said yes! I didn't know what my parents would think but soon found out. My dad had been out of town going to school for training in the ministry. When he came home we gathered the family in the living room and told them our news. My dad cried and cried.

Where Ora & Vie Met

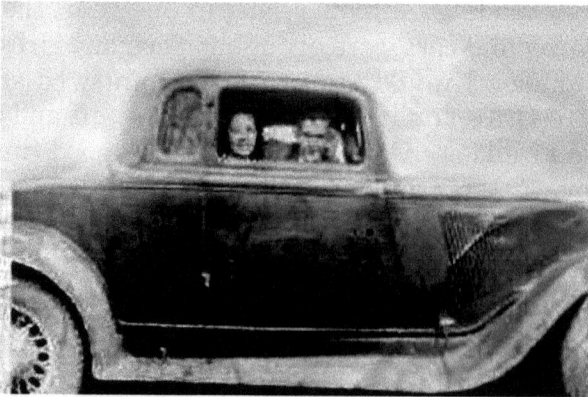

Violet and Ora Taken Easter Sunday, April 12, 1936

Ora August 26, 1936

Writing this story had some unanswered questions for me. I have tried to write as my mother wrote but listening to all the details I feel that some things have been left out.

Her marriage didn't seem as happy as she first wrote it to be. And why would my grandfather cry if he knew that my mother was marrying a man with a job and someone that would take care of her. After all he didn't really see the need for her to go to school and didn't even push the issue of working. Later I will explain my theory of what happened the summer of 1936.

It was a very simple wedding. We got married at my house and my dad performed the ceremony through many tears. At 7:00

P.M. on October 15, I married Ora Melton Stapleton. We had some friends at the house for the wedding. I borrowed Evelyn's blue dress and she didn't seem happy about that at all. She didn't want me to get married either.

Evelyn stood up with us along with my principal's daughter Leaona Hatfield. There were no flowers, no announcements and no ring! We were married. I was young and dumb.

The next day, dad borrowed money from his friend and took mom, Evelyn and I to Terre Haute, Indiana to buy me some clothes. We left Teen in school. She got mad! She came home from school at noon and tore up the house. She turned over chairs, took all the clothes out of the washer and threw them everywhere and Lula Christeen had herself a huge temper fit.

It sounded like this marriage was not planned as we had always heard it was. I have always wondered why they needed to go get clothes so far away after the wedding. What kind of clothes where they buying and why was the youngest child left out of all the details?

After my shopping spree in Terre Haute, Ora and I left to return to his family in Laconia, Indiana. This was also my home where my aunt Vie still lived. I stayed with my aunt that whole week. I knew we were going to go to his sister Agnes's house and I hated the thought of that. She was known to be so perfect and she was. On Saturday night of the first week of marriage, the friends and family there in the country gave us a kitchen shower. One hundred and thirty people came to the shower. I was so young and foolish. I really didn't know what to do. I said thank you and shyly acted as if I knew all about the stuff everyone was giving us. That night all the men gave Ora a shivery. They took him out and rode him through town and played pranks on him. A shivery is when all the people in town find the bride and groom and make loud noises under their bedroom window on the first night of marriage. Ours was a little different. The men took Ora out and I guess they even got him drunk. I don't remember all the details. I really didn't care as long as he was OK and still alive.

Violet wanted freedom from Ona and his strict rules. She felt that getting married would bring her this freedom. She was blind with love. So many times as Christians we become blind to sin and lust for the freedom of doing our own thing. Many of us find out that following your heart isn't always wise. God has a plan for our life. Remember to pray and ask for guidance.

Proverbs 16:9

A man's heart deviseth his way; but the Lord directeth his steps.

Newlyweds

The next day we left Laconia and headed for Louisville, Kentucky. I was scared to death. I had never been across the bridge. I had a sad feeling, not knowing what to expect. I was so impressed with all the lights and streets crowded with cars. I was use to small towns and I had never seen such a big place in my life. What an experience I had waiting for me. We ended our journey at 18th and Dumesnil Street. This was where his sister lived and Ora had been living for the last few years of his life. The house was a big Victorian house built in the early 1800s. The rooms were big and cold. Many families lived in this big house on separate floors. We had a room and sometimes families shared bathrooms. I had never seen a flushing toilet in my life. This was so new and fascinating to me. I was not comfortable with his sister. We only stayed there for two weeks.

Ora's uncle, Clyde Stapleton, had a three room house on 32nd and Young Street. He offered it to us. The rent was cheap and we finally had a place of our own. We lived in the front of the house and another couple lived in the back part of the house. We still had to share a bathroom and we had to go through their kitchen to get there. We had a little stove to cook on and to keep us warm. Our furniture consisted of a bed, dresser, table and two chairs. This was home! I didn't have anything to cook with, so the first Saturday after we moved in, Agnes and I went to the dime store and bought what we needed.

I was excited. Being a new bride, I couldn't wait for Ora to be a part of this gathering process. Ora only worked to noon on Saturday so he promised to meet us and help me pick out some new things for our little love nest. We waited and waited and waited but no Ora. Several hours later, he came home half drunk. What a surprise to this green little country girl. I had never had a drink and never knew anyone that did drink. He never explained anything to me. We just went back to that little room and quietly fell asleep. I was so confused. Why would he do this? Where did he go? What was going on here?

The next time he got drunk, he didn't even come home from work. He left me all alone. I didn't know if he was alright or what was going on. I didn't know anyone in Louisville except his Uncle Clyde and his sister. His sister always took his side so I chose to walk from Young Street to 18th and Wilson to his uncle's house. This was a long walk. Remember, I was stuck there all day without a car or phone. Uncle Clyde would give me something to eat and assure me that everything would be alright as he drove me home. Later I realized that Uncle Clyde probably knew where he was and who he was with.

Psalm 68:9,10

You gave abundant showers, O God; You refreshed Your weary inheritance. Your people settled in it and from Your bounty, O God, You provided for the poor.

The 1937 Flood

Now here come the answers to all my questions concerning the wedding.

Writing in her own words, Violet admits,

I got pregnant when we first moved to Louisville. Many times I went to bed hungry and sick. The 1937 flood came to Louisville. Everyone was so afraid of what would happen to their homes. We had nowhere to go. Every day it rained, and people in the west end of Louisville had to find a place to go.

Agnes called me and said, "Violet, you all need to leave as soon as you can. Tell Ora that we are going to move to a friend's house in Anchorage, Kentucky. They have enough room for two more. Gather your things and we will be by to get you in the truck."

Curt and Agnes helped us gather food and clothing and we all headed to Anchorage. Now I was pregnant, sick and had no idea where Anchorage, Kentucky was. It seemed like it took us forever to get there.

I was scared and worried that Ora would leave me for one of his nights out.

Louisville was covered with water. People were taken from their homes in boats. Louisville made news all over the radio. My parents were about crazy. They couldn't hear from me and had no idea if I was dead or alive. The telephone lines were down and I couldn't call out for a week. When I finally called to tell them what we had been through, my mother cried. We had to take Typhoid shots at the doctors' office in Anchorage. As soon as the water went down, we went back to the country and stayed for awhile. I was so glad to see my family and Ora's family. Agnes went home and found out that she had six inches of water in her house. She lost everything she owned. When we went home we had water but we didn't have much to lose.

The day we went home I started cramping and called the doctor to come to the house. The doctor ordered me to bed but it didn't help. I had a miscarriage and lost the baby. At three and a half months.

The doctor said it could have been the shots or I remember pulling up on kindling to put in our little stove. The Dr. wasn't sure what started the birth. I had the baby right there in the house. It was a little girl. (The baby was fully developed enough to know the sex of the baby. Was she pregnant when they got married? It is a secret that her sisters Evelyn and Teen would take to their graves). Ora put her in a brown bag and buried her in the back yard.

It was really a blessing. God was taking care of the situation in his own way. That baby would have been through hell with me. I went from the house to the hospital and they gave me a DNC. I got very sick and my Mom and Dad came to the hospital. I don't know how my parents got the money but the hospital bill was paid. I know I will meet that baby in heaven. My Mother told me God would finish making her up there and I would know her.

Jeremiah 29:11

"For I know the plans I have for you, Plans to prosper you not to harm you. Plans to give you hope and a future."

1937 Flood

Moving Forward

Well, we left that little one room house and moved into the next hell hole. It had two rooms and was located at 2205 Jefferson Street. We went to a furniture store on Market Street and bought some furniture for $3.00 a week. The house had no inside toilet or bath. The other two rooms in the house were rented to two nice people.

Ora never stopped drinking. I now realize that he had a big problem. Most nights he would go out for a drink before coming home. Week-ends were the worst. I did my own investigation. I listened for names of people he worked with. I asked questions about where they lived and the kinds of cars they drove. I learned where they like to hang out on weekends. A neighbor couple would help me find him when he didn't come home. One Friday night we found him upstairs at a friend's house shooting craps. I went up the stairs and knocked on the door. Boy, was he mad. All the men threw dice and money under a rug and, baby, did I leave. I was so dumb. He didn't ever hit me or anything, but he let me have it verbally when he came home drunk.

I found out that he got paid every Friday. The money never made it home. Sometimes he never made it home on Fridays. I was really hungry. When he didn't come home I would borrow twenty-five cents from the man next door and go across the street and get an R.C. for five cents, a sandwich and candy bar for fifteen cents. Boy did I hate to see Fridays come. He wouldn't mind giving me money but he never had any left after his drinking weekends. Once I can remember that my mom and dad called to say they were coming for the weekend. I was so upset. We had no food in the ice box. I called him at work and told him to borrow some money from his twin brother and be sure that he made it home in time for us to go get groceries. He was good. We pulled it off. He came home and didn't leave to drink, but I know he was not happy. I soon learned to be outside of the Tobacco Company next to his car when he got off work on Fridays. I had to take a bus to get downtown.

We found the cutest three room cottage on Woodlawn close to Parkland school. I fixed it up so cute, and Ora stopped drinking for one year. We were happy again. The happiest we had ever been in our married life. We both learned that we really loved each other. We enjoyed doing things together like playing cards with other couples. This didn't last for long. We had to move from our little dream house. The people that owned the house wanted to sell it. They would have sold it to us for 350.00 dollars down. We had to say no because we didn't have the money. His sister Agnes could have helped us, but we couldn't get help from anyone. Broken hearted we had to move.

Looking for a place to live, we moved back to the first house of Uncle Clyde's. This time Ora's twin brother and his wife Leona were renting the whole house. We lived with them until we could find another house to live in. Leona and I went to work at a pickle factory for twenty-five cents an hour. Leona and I drove to the pickle factory together. Ira and Ora went to work together. I worked there for two years helping to earn enough money to find a house to live in.

In 1944, we rented an old house for fifteen dollars a month. It was a fine house. It was located on Cypress Street near Parkland. Parkland was the rich part of town in the 1800s. It was still a nice neighborhood with big old Victorian houses lined up in a row. Huge shaded trees decorated the green yards with flower lined walkways leading to the wrap around porches. Parkland was a small little town all its own. There was a bank, dime store, shoe store, movie theater, drug store, A&P grocery, diner, clothes store and anything you needed. Our house was just down the street in the heart of Parkland. I could walk to get anything I needed.

We lived upstairs at this beautiful house. An older lady lived downstairs with her son. It seemed like we lived there *forever. Although it was nice I still wanted a house of my own. The old lady would not let us run water when we wanted and she kept a watch on the heat as well. She was always bossing us around. It made us miserable. It didn't help having Ora coming home drunk late at night. He was so different when he drank. I didn't know what to expect. Sometimes he would be angry. Not knowing what kind of mood he would be in, I would hide behind the couch most of the time sleeping there all night long.*

Money was scarce and Ora was back to his old drinking ways. I was determined to work and make money. I went to work at the Hines Ketchup factory and made more money. It was an awful place. Women were not treated equal in the factory. We had to grab hot bottles off the line with thin gloves. Our hands were burnt and peeling, so we would wrap them in gauzes to keep the blusters from bleeding through the gloves. The heat was sickening. Many women would pass out from the heat of the scalding machines and the lack of air flowing through the hot factory.

We got together and formed a union. I was president of our union. We expressed our concerns and presented them to the company. Women didn't have a voice but we tried to make the best of a bad situation.

One night I went to a union meeting which was held next to a big dance hall. I rode with a girlfriend to the meeting. When we left there, I spotted Ora's car. I wanted to investigate.

"Hey Joan, wait a minute. Could you drive over there next to that car? I think it's my husbands' car."

"Oh, Violet, what would he be doing here," replied Joan. "You must be mistaken. Come on, let's go home."

"No! I just have to see for myself. Drive over there and let me take a look."

We rode around the parking lot and I got out and looked inside the car. "It's his car alright. He's inside the dance hall. I wonder who he's with."

"Come on, Violet, let it be," said Joan.

I replied, "Are you kidding? I have to find out who he's with, and the only way to do that is to do some dancing of my own."

I walked into the bar like I owned the place, and I spotted Ora with another woman. I stood there and made sure he saw me before I left. He was drinking a lot that night. Looked like four or five bottles of beer on the table. I left and went back out to the car.

"Take me home, Joan," I insisted. "I just want to go home." Joan took me straight home and I was crying inside as I walked up the steps and opened the door. Soon he came home looking for me. I was getting undressed and just had my slip on when he walked in the house. I was afraid of him so I grabbed his keys out of his hand and ran ahead of him, got in the car and drove to my friend's house to spend the night. When I got there I realize that I was still in my slip.

Wisdom in the Word kept Violet safe and even-tempered.

Proverbs 18:10

The name of the Lord is a strong tower; the righteous run to it and are safe.

Women and Booze

His drinking did not stop. Each time he got drunk he would tell me he was sorry and it wouldn't happen again. My love for him allowed me to believe his sorry words. He would go for two weeks and never drink a drop. He had good intentions but the addiction would not allow him to live a life free from the sin he had drowned himself in since he was a teenager of fourteen.

He had several girlfriends. All the ladies wanted to be with him. He loved the attention of being pursued by women. He was good-looking, had a great personality and he knew it. I soon learned there were many women and I made it my business to learn their names. I talked to people that worked with him and followed him when I could find a friend to drive as my spy. Most of them worked with him. They all liked to go out after work. I found out where they went to drink. I walked into bars to confront him. Each time he gave me this poor pathetic "I am sorry," and I would crumble to forgiveness.

I was young and dumb and in some strange way I loved him very much. When he wasn't drinking he was my best friend. He was a lot of fun and everyone wanted to be his friend. We enjoyed going to the country on weekends to visit his family. He had nephews that played music and Ora loved to play the harmonica and sing with the boys. He also liked to play cards and drink a little with the brothers-in-law. This type of drinking was harmless. He loved me being there with him and his sisters. His sisters liked to cook. We would make large Sunday meals and sit outside under a big old shade tree. I knew everyone around there. Some of them were my cousins. My aunts, uncles and cousins still lived in Laconia and we all visited when we got together. It was lots of fun. His family liked to laugh, sing and eat. We made candy, pies and homemade ice cream on hot summer days. They were all good cooks. When we went to the country he even went to church with me and the whole family. He also went with me to see my parents. He was always a gentleman when he was around my preacher dad. I loved those times we had together. My sister, Evelyn, knew about his drinking because she shared the same secret with her soon-to-be husband. Sometimes they would slip away together and have a drink. We both held our breath hoping that they would come home and be decent around our parents.

I am sure Ona and Bessie knew that Violet, Evelyn, and Teen were struggling with their home life as preacher's children. Everyone in town expected too much from them. Ona was always preaching about what not to do. There was a short list of what they could do. The girls learned that their responsibility was to please their parents. What they failed to teach them was to respect God and his word. Ona was a good preacher, but I think he preached only how he believed. Each girl had to find out for herself that married life was not as glamorous as it seemed. It was a ticket away from home and the church, but not a ticket they needed for happiness.

For many of us our backgrounds have been very painful. We feel hurt, angry and rejected. We tend to hide these feelings because we feel guilty or disrespectful to our parents. I have learned through therapy that it's okay to admit your anger. The only person you need to obey is God. I wish the sisters, could have found happiness in God's own time. Then again, I might not be here to write this story.

Ephesians 1:11
In Him we were also chosen, having been predestined according to the plan of Him who works out everything in conformity with the purpose of His will.

Army Days

In 1942 while still living on Cypress Street, Ora got drafted in the army.

I remember it like it was yesterday. I was sitting in the porch swing on a nice September day when the postman came and said. "I am giving you something you won't like. He handed me the envelope marked US Army. I opened it and waited for Ora to come home. He walked up the steps and sat next to me on the swing. I was crying.

"What's the matter?" he said.

"You got your letter today. Looks like Uncle Sam needs your help."

He read the letter and assured me that everything was going to be alright.

My brothers-in-laws got the same kind of letter. World War II was in full swing and more men were being enlisted into the service. His twin brother Ira went with the Navy and was assigned to a ship headed to England.

Ora didn't leave until January of the next year. They gave him a party at Brown and Williams Tobacco Company. He got lots of money for gifts. He put it in his back pocket and patted it and said, "Boy, wouldn't you like to have this." I couldn't think of anything to say back and I didn't get any of his money either.

The day came for him to go to the train station. He said goodbye at home and he wouldn't let me go with him. His brother-in-law Curt took him and I cried the night away in that big old house all by myself. Who knows, he might have had a girlfriend at the train station waiting to say good-bye.

When I think of all the things I went through to stay married to that man. I never gave up!

Many times I knelt by that old red couch and prayed for a Christian home and for him to become a Christian. I needed money and I couldn't just sit at home and cry. I got up one morning and walked to the grocery. I charmed the manager at the store and by the end of the day I had me a job at the A&P grocery store in Parkland. Ora left me the car and I could go anywhere I wanted to go. It was the first time in my life that I had money and a car. I could have spent time traveling back and forth to Indiana, but I wanted to work and make money. There was a lot of snow that winter and I didn't have a lot of friends to run with so I was happy just to work. I would walk to work and walk home at lunch to see if I had a letter from Ora. He did write me. I was so lonely. His letters made life worth living. Can you believe that I longed to see him after all I had been through? I was so dumb. I was in love.

He was stationed in Augusta, Georgia. He was there about three weeks and started calling me to come down and see him. I said no each time until one day in March. He called begging me to come to Georgia. He said he missed me so much he just couldn't stand it. He had it all planned out. He said I could come with three other girls who had husbands stationed with him. I was so dumb. I gave up my good paying job and agreed to visit him. I went into town and bought some new clothes. During WWII we all had to sacrifice a lot. We had ration books for such things as shoes, gas, sugar, tires, clothing and many more popular items needed to keep us comfortable. There was a shortage of nylon so we would take a black pen and draw a line down the back of our legs to look like seams in our nylons.

The army wives had a check for fifty dollars a month to live on. This was the first time I had new clothes, but had little freedom to buy them using ration stamps.

I talked with the other girls on the phone and we shared what we would be wearing so we would know each other when we met at the bus station. We met and left for Georgia on March 17, 1942. It seemed like it took us forever to get to Georgia. I could hardly stay in my seat as the excitement of traveling on a big bus and seeing Ora flowed through my body. It was nice to have other girls to talk to that were in the same situation as I was. We couldn't stop talking about *our husbands. We were certainly best friends by the time we finished our trip. The men got us some rooms and met us at the bus station. I was so excited to see Ora. I saw him as soon as we pulled up to the bus station. My, he was in that uniform and looked so handsome. Love just flowed all over me, again. I couldn't wait for him to hold me in his arms. It was as if nothing was ever wrong with our relationship. He got to leave the base two nights a week and on weekends. I lived for the time we had together. Life was great!*

Marie and Irene were the names of the other ladies who were staying with me in Georgia. We all had good times together cooking, sharing, and going places as couples. This was fun for awhile, but I was use to making my own money and I didn't want to get that poor again. I got a job right away at JC Penney's. I really didn't like working there, but I stayed for the money. My main complaint was the way people were treated.

Being a Christian from a small country town, I wasn't use to the way black people were treated. I remember waiting on a black woman and called her a lady. Boy, did I get bowled out! The manger said, "Don't ever let me hear you call a black woman a lady. Down here we call them niggers." This was the way everyone talked down there. I remember another time when the man who lived next door to us asked me where his wife went. I replied, "She is in the back yard with the lady that works for you." He immediately called me on the carpet.

"She is a nigger and don't let me hear you call her a lady. I know about niggers and I have even killed some of them."

What a scare he gave me! I couldn't believe the way people talked. I later saw a place there in town where blacks were sold. There were chains still hanging with the concrete blocks. This is where they were auctioned off to the highest bidder. When we rode the bus the blacks rode in the back of the bus. Signs with white drinking water fountains and white only restrooms were everywhere. Just think this all took place in 1942. How could this be?

We spent one year in Georgia and along with working at

J.C. Penny's I had another offer to work for a pie maker lady. I took the job and delivered pies every day. I saved enough money, along with some borrowed from my sister Evelyn, to buy me a 1943 Plymouth. To save money, Marie and I moved into another apartment that was cheaper.

Soon Ora's company was sent to Alabama for more training. Driving my new car, I took five other girls in my car to join our husbands in Alabama. Each girl gave me money and helped pay for the gas. We found rooms and a place to stay near the base. We all looked for jobs and found no one was hiring. Luckily it wasn't long before the men were sent back to Georgia to pack up and get ready to go overseas. I went back to Georgia and I got my job back. I worked there until Ora was sent overseas. I was never afraid of hard work.

Right before Ora left to go overseas, I found out that I was three months pregnant. I realized that I would have to return home without him being there to support me. Sadly Marie and I drove from Augusta, Georgia home to Louisville. The men were shipped out and we had no idea how long they would be gone.

Violet and Ora 1943

2 Peter 38:8,9

But do not forget this one thing, dear friends: With the Lord a day is like a thousand years and a thousand years are like a day. The Lord is not slow in keeping His promise as some understand slowness. He is patient with you, not wanting anyone to perish, but everyone to come to repentance.

Back Home in Indiana

I went back home to Center Point, Indiana to live with my mom and dad. My dad was very upset with me when he found out that I was pregnant. He said, "Seven years you have waited for him to get his act together and now he is going overseas and leaving you with a baby to take care of."

I was so sick during the pregnancy. I didn't need a daily sermon. I couldn't wait until the day that I would deliver my baby and be back home on my own.

On January 11, 1945, my little girl was born. I wanted a little black headed girl and I got my wish. We named her Janice and my mom named her Kaye. I so wished Ora could have been there with me to see this beautiful, perfect little girl. She was born in Brazil Indiana and my mother, father, and sisters along with the other relatives were very excited for me. We stayed with my parents along with my sister Christeen and her young baby. My brother-in-law, JR, was also in the army along with Ora. I am sure it wasn't easy for my parents having us all living there, but it was also hard on us.

We would listen to the radio every night to see what was happening with the troops. I was so lonesome there in Indiana. I didn't know anyone. Time passed so slowly and there was nothing to do but wish I was back in Louisville with Ora.

I was now getting seventy-five dollars a month because I had a child to support. I saved my rations on gas stamps so I could pass the time away by visiting relatives. I would go to the country to see my aunt Vie and up to Louisville to visit with Ora's sister Agnes. I would also save my rations to send Ora lots of cigarettes and soap that he requested every time he wrote me. I would box up lots of goodies and send them to him when we were allowed to know where the company was staying. I later found out that the men would trade these particular items for sexual favors when they landed in France. How nice of me to sacrifice my food and clothing for his pleasure. He also brought me home a little disease as a souvenir from his trip. I didn't know for weeks what was going on until I went to the doctor and we both had to be treated.

Because of her unique personal experiences, Violet was deceived by love. She forgave him for all of his sinning ways because she was too insecure to face reality. He played the game and she pretended it didn't happen.

Violet's faith in God allowed her to believe that Ora was going to someday surrender to God and change his life. This was her daily prayer. She was never aware that God was in control of her life and in God's time prayer would be answered.

You cannot save your love ones. Each person must be convicted by the Holy Spirit and long for a personal relationship with Jesus Christ.

1 Peter 5:6,7
Humble yourselves, therefore, under God's mighty hand, that He may lift you up in due time. Cast all your anxiety on Him because He cares for you.

Ora Comes Home

Janice was afraid of all men. The only man she would go to was my dad. We would take her to church around men and she would cry whenever a man spoke to her. This really worried me. I took her to see Ora's twin brother Ira when he came home on leave. I thought she might warm up to him. She took one look at him and cried her eyes out. This frightened me even more. What am I going to do if she cries when she sees her daddy?

After eighteen lonesome months the day finally arrived. Ora was coming home to stay. The war was over. It was the best news America had received in months. Janice and I met him at the bus station in Brazil, Indiana. There he was all dressed up in that uniform with his raincoat and duffel bag looking so handsome. Janice was in her baby seat dressed like a doll. She was sound asleep. He opened the door and took a long look at her. He drove the car back to Mom and Dad's and carried her in the house and put her down on the bed. He looked her over real good and said, "Let me see what I have here." When she woke up he picked her up and she went right to him without crying. She loved him from the very start and he was wild about her. We spent the night at my parents' and headed back to Louisville the next day. We had kept that old two-room apartment on Cypress Street and no one had lived there for two years. It was so dirty and full of smoke. People back then smoked and burned coal in their stoves to keep them warm. We cleaned and cleaned all week long. Janice was a busy two-year-old. She would get so dirty until we could get everything cleaned up. Ora got his job back at Brown and Williams. I didn't work. I was so crazy about Janice I just knew no one could take care of her like I could. She was a very active baby. The old lady, who lived downstairs, would complain if she cried. We needed a new place to live. I started looking for another place close by. We didn't have much money so it would take a while before we could move to a house by ourselves.

Janice started kindergarten down the street where we lived on Cypress. The school was Parkland Baptist School. I would take her to school and start back home, and she would follow me back home crying all the way. I would have to take her back to school and make sure she was in her class. She cried almost every day. I couldn't take leaving her in tears. She went until Christmas and I took her out. The next year she was in first grade. First grade was better. She made friends and started to enjoy school.

It was hard to see your baby grow up and become independent of your assistants. Mom was always attached to her children.

Just like a new mother, the Lord will not forget us. He sees our trials and promises hope for the future.

Isaiah 49:15
Can a mother forget the baby at her breast and have no compassion on the child she has borne?

Opening a Business

We found a house on Hale Street still located in Parkland. It wasn't a mansion but we fixed it up. It had two rooms and a bath upstairs. We rented it out for fifteen dollars a week. We didn't have the money for it so I borrowed $500.00 from my aunt Vie for the down payment for one year. Then later I went to the bank in Parkland and borrowed $500 more to pay off my aunt. I was still upset at the thought of leaving Janice with someone after school, however we needed money and I knew I had to work. In 1949, I started a day care center for children. I kept them in my home from 4:00 in the afternoon until 12:00 at night. I was surprised at the amount of money this brought into the family. Soon I had lots of request for day care and I opened my house in the day and started keeping kids from 6:00 in the morning until the evening.

Ora helped me build my business and added on to the back of the house so we could start a real day care. Even though he loved Janice and me, Ora was back at his old job and back to his old tricks. His weekends became his drinking days and his money was soon gone. He was still running around with ladies from the factory. I was getting lots of information from people who knew us. I found pictures in his wallet. I had children in the nursery whose parents worked with Ora. They confirmed information that I was hoping was hearsay. He was telling everyone that he was separated from his wife. He was so afraid his lie would catch up with him that he hid and sometimes refused to go places in public with us. He would sit on the front porch, and when a car passed he would scoot down in the swing pretending to comb his hair so his face couldn't be seen. He had learned how to park his car down the block from a bar or house so I couldn't see it.

One Saturday night at 1:00 in the morning someone knocked on our door, and Ora answered it with me following behind. He was caught in his lie and lost that girlfriend. Somehow it was my fault so he yelled at me and packed his clothes and went to his sister's house to spend the night. He often ran to her when he was mad or drunk. What a life. I was getting use to his lies and like always he would sober up and be sorry the next day.

Ora liked to hunt and fish. I would go fishing with him and we would take Janice with us. Janice loved being with her dad. He taught her how to fish, shoot a BB gun and hunt night crawlers. She even worked with him on cars in the garage. It was good that we could fish together as a family, but his love for hunting and fishing also took him out of town to the country by himself. He could use this as an excuse to run around and drink without getting caught.

I always tried to go to the country with him on weekends. This would be the only way we could be together as a family. It also kept him sober. I would plan any event to keep him home with us. Even though we would make it through the weekends, there was always Monday and back to work in that hell-hole of a factory where everyone was sleeping with everyone else. I would get lots of hang-up calls at night and some drinking buddies would call looking for Ora. It never stopped. As bad as it was, I was still hopeful that someday we would be a real family. I never stopped praying.

Soon after Ora was home from the army he changed jobs and went to work at The American Tobacco Company. This was a new company in town that was an extension of The Brown and Williamson Company. He was hired on to fix the machines. I was excited about the change. It was more money and hopefully a change from the wild group of people he worked with. He joined the company ball team and made a lot of new friends. Janice and I would go watch him play ball. Life seemed to be going better for our little family.

Pictures from the Nursery

A Baby Sister for Janice

Janice liked all the kids in the nursery and she was determined that she had to have a little baby sister. Of course she always got what she wanted. Ora had stopped drinking for awhile and I felt it was time to maybe have that baby sister for Janice. On October 3, 1953 our second daughter was born. She was a beautiful baby girl. Ora was there and told Janice as soon as he knew that the baby was born. Thank goodness it was a girl. Janice named her Linda Sue after a child in the nursery. I never saw a more thrilled eight year old when she saw that baby sister. She came to the hospital to get us. She wanted to do everything for her. Ora loved her too. He couldn't wait to see her and hold her when he got home from work. I would dress her up in the afternoons right before he came home so she would look beautiful for him. As she got older she would wait on the porch for her daddy to come home from work.

The nursery was doing wonderful. We began to grow and I needed lots of help to run the day to day business. I hired girls from the country to come up to live in our upstairs and in return they would work in the nursery. Linda was very fond of Jo, one of the first employees I hired. I had it hard taking care of the business and being a mother, so Jo made sure that Linda got all her needs met. When Jo left, Ora's niece Wilma and her husband Jack came to live with us. This was a very happy time for all of us. Jack was stationed in Fort Knox and Wilma would help me in the daycare. Again she and Jack unofficially adopted Linda. I was busy taking children to school and doing the grocery shopping daily for the nursery. I did it all. I took care of children from morning till night. Ora was my best reference at the tobacco company. A lot of women kept their jobs when they were hired on during the war. It almost took two parents working to keep food on the table. I charged less than ten dollars a week. So now you see why women continued to stay in the workforce.

I also had a person who would come in and clean for me on Saturdays. We were doing well in our business, and Ora was working overtime. I had two sisters that worked for me and took care of my baby, Linda. I worked day and night growing my business. We were able to buy a new Oldsmobile. We had rental property and money for the first time in my life. We bought a new washer and dryer and paid for it a little at a time and even a new deep freeze. I could see us going places.

It was 1956 and I was happy with a home a business and two beautiful children. I had no clue that soon my life was about to fall apart. I was not attending church like I was taught. I didn't want to go without Ora. There was a little Methodist church a few blocks away and Ora was asked to play on their ball team. I remember visiting the church once and met a lot of people who were friendly to me. They were always inviting me to attend the church activities. I got a visit from one of the members and when he learned that I was a preacher's daughter he asked me to come teach a Sunday school class. I knew in my heart I needed to be in church, but still again I wasn't willing to give up my weekends with Ora. Weekends were family time and I looked forward to going to the country.

When Linda was eight months old, she became very ill. She was having a hard time breathing, and would not take her bottle. We rushed her to the hospital and they said there was something wrong with her lungs. The doctors took my baby away from me and immediately rushed her off to the X-ray department leaving me there by myself. It was at this point in my life I needed God. I prayed, looking at that statue of Mary in the hospital, and I asked God to please save my little girl. I started making promises to Him. I confessed my sins and I promised Him that I would go to the Methodist church and teach Bible school on Sundays. I promised that I would take the girls to church and raise them as Christians. I knew that God was real and I knew that He would comfort my soul. I left everything in His hands.

Soon the Doctor came out and told us that she had something in her lung that looked like a safety pin. They put her to sleep and sucked parts of baby food out of the lung. We both recovered in the hospital overnight. When everything was back to normal, I realized that I had a promise to fulfill. I called the Methodist church and took on the job as a Sunday school teacher. I begged Ora to go to church with us but as always he wasn't interested. I knew I had to keep my promise. I went to church every Sunday with my girls and even sang in the choir. I met a lot of good friends there and so did Janice.

Galatians 4:22-23

For it is written that Abraham had two sons, one by the slave woman and the other by the free woman. His son by the free woman was born as the result of a promise.

Another Bump in the Road

Ora's Sundays were also filled with joy. Little did I know that he had met a new woman at the American Tobacco Company and he was visiting with her when we were at church. I saw his car over there one Sunday and I ran into the back of it. Linda ended up with a bloody nose and his girlfriend's sister called the police. Ora told them it was just a family problem and they left us alone. Janice got out and pulled the hair of the girlfriend's sister who was now calling all of us names. What a mess! It turned out that her sister was about the same age as Janice and was attending the same school. Her sister would call Janice names at school and make fun of her.

Ora started his old habits of drinking and staying out late at nights. Some nights he would come home drunk and angry. I was afraid for the girls and myself. I didn't like him when he was loud and drunk. Even though he never hit me, I hit him several times. I was just angry that he could mess up our life like this. How dare he take everything we had worked for and throw it all away on beer and women! He was always sorry and he loved his little girls so much, but he was torn between the old life style and his new one.

I was quite familiar with his pattern of drinking and coming home late at night. I found out that there was one woman he was seen with on a regular basis.

One of my friends that worked at the factory with him found out her name and I started my investigation. I followed him when I could. I found out where she lived. I found his car parked down the street from her house. I would take the girls out of bed at night and wrap them in blankets and go out looking for him.

I once looked in a window and caught him playing cards

with her and some of our so-called friends. The man recognized me and said, "Oh, my God! Ora, there's Violet." He got so mad he came after me. I ran for the car and that night I locked the girls and me upstairs so he couldn't start something.

I would often lock us upstairs when Ora was out drinking. I would take food and water upstairs and felt safe from the drunken rage that might take place when he came home. This became a routine and an obsession of mine to follow Ora at night. I always took the girls with me. When I would find his car I would get out and investigate. Once Janice decided to get out of the car and follow me. She saw him with this woman inside her house. She was so mad that she was going to throw a big log through the window. I had to stop her and go home.

I really didn't care that this was affecting my pre-teen daughter. I wasn't even thinking about the kids' feelings. I was so selfish that I just wanted to confront him and let him know that he wasn't going to pull this stuff over on me. I knew his game and I was tired of it. He said he wasn't doing anything wrong, just having fun with some people from work.

I would lock the door so he couldn't get in, and he would start leaving the window unlocked so he could climb in the window. I continued to follow him and one night I saw him dancing with her in a joint near our house. Finally, I confronted her. I found out her name and her phone number. I called her on the phone and told her who I was. She said that she thought that we were separated. I told her that she could come and look in my house and see that his clothes were still there.

We matched the stories that he was giving both of us. She found out that he was lying to her. I thought that confronting this with her and him would make things change. He promised that he would stop seeing her and said he loved me more than anything.

He quit his job at the factory and we bought a hardware store on 16th Street. He was a hard worker and this seemed to be the answer to saving our marriage. Little did I know, she soon started visiting the hardware store and was begging him to leave me and marry her. I found out that they went to Gatlinburg, Tennessee together. I didn't find out for a year. I sent him to Florida with my father because he seemed depressed. Little did I know that he was depressed because she was begging him to move out of our house.

On the trip to Florida he called her and soon cut the trip short because he wasn't feeling well. He couldn't wait to see her. He couldn't find a way to get away from home. It was January and Janice's birthday. I sent him out for groceries and he didn't show up until Sunday three days later. He spent the weekend with his mistress. What a rat. I must give him credit, when he came home he did have the groceries. Ha!

2 Thessalonians 1:6-8

God is just: He will pay back trouble to those who trouble you and give relief to you who are troubled and to us as well. This will happen when the Lord Jesus is revealed from Heaven in blazing fire with his powerful angels. He will punish those who do not know God and do not obey the gospel of our Lord Jesus.

Broke Again

We lost our money in the hardware store and almost lost our pants. We were behind on every bill we owed. Ora was drinking and not working. An insurance company came for Ora's signature on a policy that was not paid. I lied and said he was sick in the back room and had Janice to sign his signature saying he would pay by a certain date. This gave me time to figure out what I needed to do. He wasn't coming home nights at all. I had no idea where he was. He said he was staying with his sister and his sister had no idea where he was. He got a job as a cab driver. He came by to see me and the girls. He said he had to go away to think things over. He wanted to change everything and wanted us to move to Indiana. He said he needed to get away from the city. I let him come back home once again and we started to look for a home in Indiana. We found a farm that was just across the river and we talked about selling the daycare and making a change in everything. I was crazy enough to be sucked into the big scam. Just as everything was back to normal and I was excited about the thought of him being home, it wasn't long until he messed up again. He came home drunk and I had finally had it. I told him to pack his bags and move out. He didn't even fight about it. He put all of his clothes in his pajama bottoms as the girls and I stood by watching. Four-year-old Linda looked at him so pitifully and said, "Daddy, what are you going to sleep in?" I couldn't help but to cry. He left that night and I finally knew that it was all over. I cried for days. I couldn't even begin to face reality. I was glad I had good workers in the daycare. The girls that worked for me took care of my kids. Janice took care of Linda at night. I would forget to feed them at night. It was the worst thing that had ever happened to me. I was sitting on the porch swing one night looking so unhappy when my neighbor asked me what was wrong. I told him that I needed to get a divorce but didn't have any money. Babe and Emma, my neighbors, loaned me the money, and in 1958 I was seeing a lawyer and the divorce was in process.

Ora didn't fight over one thing. He even gave me the car along with the house, and everything in it. I asked for child support and he agreed to pay child support as long as he could see the girls whenever he wanted. I asked that he never take them around his girlfriend. He granted my wishes and they never saw her until his death.

To my surprise Ora married right away. His new wife was pregnant. Ora must have known this when he left me. I suddenly knew this must have been the reason that he was so generous with all of our belongings. The week he got married he stopped by my house and told me he had just made the biggest mistake of his life. He said he was sorry and that he still loved me and the girls. Somehow this did not make a big difference. I didn't feel sorry for him. I was still feeling sorry for myself. I still loved him.

The hardware store was put up for sale by the court house because we couldn't make payments. My lawyer, Mr. Kellerman, helped me get it back. No one bid against me and I got it at a low price. I also had the rental property, and we traded it and I ended up with three thousand dollars in the bank. I now had seventeen kids in the daycare.

The word of God tells us that our hearts don't have to stay that way. God can make a difference in your heart and life. Mom was in financial straits, agonizing over a broken relationship. She felt like a failure because her husband cheated on her. Thank God she had a strong faith that would allow her to make it through these hard times.

Jeremiah 17:9
    The heart is deceitful above all things and desperately wicked. Who can know it?

Violet Moves On

After the divorce I didn't think I ever wanted to meet another man. I was lonesome and really was afraid living alone in that big house with the girls. I went up the stairs with the girls at night and I would feel safer being locked up there until morning. I remember crying saying, "God there must be someone somewhere that will love me." I stopped feeling sorry for myself and started bowling with some girls whom I sponsored on a league. One night one of the girls told me she had someone she wanted me to meet. I wasn't interested. I was still in love and no one would ever take his place. She continued to tell me about him saying that he was a Sunday school teacher at his church and that his wife had left him for someone she worked with. Soon she convinced me to let her give him my number. He called me every night from where he worked. We would just talk and I didn't say anything about going out with him. Then one Saturday he came by and introduced himself to me. He asked me to go to Frankfort with him to deliver some papers. I said no. He said okay, but he would still keep trying to take me out. He would call on the phone to talk to me and I would go outside with the kids and tell the girls in the daycare to tell him that I wasn't there. Then one day he drove by the daycare and saw me sitting out in the yard with the kids. We started to talk and our first date was to my church Valentine party. We took Linda with us. She was just four years old.

He had two children of his own. His wife did not want the children. They lived with his mother during the evening while he was at work, and he took care of them when he wasn't working. The first time I met his children, he brought them to a dinner at my house. They were much louder than my quite Linda. One was seven and the other was six. They

went upstairs to play, and they were so loud that they
sounded like they were taking off the roof. The six-year-old
boy threw Linda's doll suite case down the steps, and
everyone at the party ran to see if the kids were all right.
Kyle got mad and took them straight home. I later learned
that they both got punished. This was not unusual for Kyle.
He was very strict with those kids. I felt sorry for them. He
was yelling at them and hitting them. I didn't say much. It
wasn't my place.

Violet stopped writing her story. She skipped the introduction of the children to our family. Later she continued expressing her feelings concerning her decision to marry.

Janice and Linda wondered why the children were always hanging around the house. Kyle and Violet hadn't been dating long and his children began to attend the daycare. Janice asked, "Mom, are the kids going to move into our house?" Violet was so coy about the whole situation. She couldn't face the truth. In her heart she hoped that they could all be family.

"Why, no! Their grandmother is sick and they are going to stay for a week."

The week ended up being day and night. It was an awful week. The kids were wild. They fought over toys and with the other kids in the daycare. They had the freedom of eating anything they wanted and they ate all the time. I guess they were hungry. Their grandmother would not feed them much. The boy (Ron) would eat so much that he would throw up when he went to bed at night. Mom's now boyfriend, Kyle, was taking advantage of a good situation. Kyle told her she was a wonderful mother and she felt sorry for the kids. She was so lonely that she started to date him on a regular basis. One night we spent the night with our aunt while Mom and Kyle went out somewhere. Daddy found out about it. He was waiting for them to arrive at my aunt's house to pick up us girls. Daddy was drunk as usual and got out of the car and wanted to beat Kyle up. They rolled around on the hill swinging at each other. Then Daddy went to his car and said he was going to get his gun. He returned with his shoe. Hearing all the noise, my uncle, came out of the house and took Daddy home. He was steaming mad that mom had found someone to date. That rage of jealousy excited mom. It wasn't long until she was going to Frankfort to get a marriage license. Mom planned a great big wedding. I am sure there were at least one hundred people there. I, along with Sara and Ron, were all dressed alike and walked down the aisle together. Janice played the piano. Mom had three attendants. Ona married her again. Mom's sisters and mother were not real happy with this big wedding. She now had two more kids to raise and she had only known this man for six months. His parents never liked Mom. Kyle was only eighteen years older than Janice. Kyle's family took part in the wedding but never accepted Mom into their family. The mother-in-law was thankful that she was relieved of her responsibilities concerning Kyle's children. She was a mean woman and never acknowledged Janice and me.

Mom continued to write her story for three years. Her health was failing and she repeated herself many times. It's been hard to make the account flow from year to year. She also left out the things that she would rather not share or remember. Continuing her story, she writes,

The date was August 8, 1959. Kyle and I were married in the big Methodist church I was attending. We left right after the wedding to go to Florida on our honeymoon. Each set of children went to stay with their own grandparents for a week. I was very lonesome for my girls. I had a horrible time on my trip. What was I thinking? This was the first time I had ever been away from Linda. Janice had stayed with her grandparents and aunts. Linda, on the other hand, was so afraid of me leaving her for good. I made sure that I never left her overnight. Not even with my sister. The week ended and I was sure glad to pick up my girls and go home. Linda cried when she saw me. I had no idea it would have affected her this way. She shook all the way home.

I was confused and my spirit was crushed. I had no idea what to expect in new situations. I was afraid that my mother was going to leave us forever just like daddy.

Proverbs 15:13
A happy heart makes the face cheerful, but heartache crushes the spirit.

A New Family

It was hard getting use to three more mouths to feed. I came home, sat on the porch next to Janice and said, "I've made the biggest mistake of my life." He was good to me but it wasn't love. I knew his kids needed someone to care for them. They were truly orphans. Somehow I hoped we would all get adjusted. The kids shared the huge bed rooms upstairs and we slept down stairs so I could open the daycare at 6:00 in the morning. Kyle continued to work odd shifts. He worked some days and some nights. I took the kids to register them in school. He didn't have much to bring to my house. All he had was a bedroom suite and a chest. I took the kids out to buy them clothes, and along with my regular school children, I piled his kids in my big old Oldsmobile and drove them all to Parkland Baptist school. Janice was in junior high school. She went on a bus or with friends. At 2:30 I had to make the rounds again to pick up everyone from school and back to work at the daycare until it now closed at 6:30 P.M. The money Kyle was making was not enough for all of us to live. I had to try and take in more children.

I was only five when we joined the families together, but I do remember that it was a big adjustment for Janice and me. We couldn't go out to eat on Fridays like we looked forward to doing. Mom and Kyle were always arguing about everything that took place in the house. If she suggested something he would always cut it down and try to act like she was dumb for even thinking on her own. Janice and I stayed together all the time. I played with his kids but Sara was so bossy like her daddy and Ron was hyper and in your face always getting into your stuff. We had to learn to share everything. I can remember always being afraid to be left alone. Mom had hired two sisters to take care of me when I was just a baby. I loved them dearly. They were the only stable thing besides, my sister, in my life.

Mom always had people living with us. A young lady and her son came to live up stairs with all of us in the fall after the wedding. She helped in the nursery. Her baby was always crying at night and we were stuffed up there like a can of sardines. We even took them on vacation with us in the station wagon. She helped with meals and cleaning. She would babysit us while they went bowling on Friday nights. It was a crazy kind of family for us. I would escape the mess by going off by myself and playing with my dolls. Sara and Ron didn't like playing dolls. They always wanted to play rough tag games and get into trouble. When their father punished them he would take off his belt and hit their legs. Meal times were the worst. Throughout the meals he would flick them behind the ears and make them sit up straight and make negative comments on how they were eating. Sometimes he would deny them food, sending them straight to bed. I was often afraid of him. His children's mother rarely called them and only sent for them by cab for just a few hours maybe once every two to three months. Mom would call her on the phone and ask her why she didn't want to keep them over night or take them on trips. She would laugh and say, "Well, Kyle wanted them so now he can raise them." It seemed that we never had a break from each other. My aunts and grandparents took Kyle's children places and treated them like they were family. They even called them Mamaw and Papaw, Aunt and Uncle and did until the day they died. Kyle's family seldom took them for the week-end or for a whole day.

Violet writes,
The house on Hale Street was not big enough for all the kids and all of us so I begin to look for a new house. The kids were going to Parkland Elementary school and it was an all black school. In the '60s schools were not integrated. The county schools were the better schools so I wanted to get our kids out of the city and into the county school system. We needed money to buy a new house. I prayed that God would find us a house and help me get the children into a good school. I took the $3,000.00 from my bank and made a down

payment on a house in Shively. This was the money from the trading of the house and hardware store. We had to keep the house in Parkland for the nursery. I took the bird dog that Ora left behind and sold it for $75.00. This made a down payment on a brown sectional for the house. Kyle and I worked day and night trying to get the house ready to move into. My brother-in-law was a carpenter and he helped us rebuild the stairs and tear out walls to make a large living room. Kyle got $1,000.00 dollars from his divorce and we used his money to buy carpet for the new house. I was giving the new address at school while we were still living in the old nursery. I would get up at 5:00 in the morning and get the kids ready to go to work with me. We would open the daycare at 6:00 A.M. and then I would take all the nursery kids and mine to school all over the city and county. At one time I had five different schools where I delivered children on a daily basis. All of them crammed into that big old Oldsmobile. I needed to make money and this was the only way we could make things work.

We moved into our new house on Noble Place and each child had his/her own room. Mary and her baby moved back in with us for awhile until she could find a place to live in Indiana. She stayed in Linda's room. Janice and Linda always slept together. Linda was afraid to sleep by herself. Kyle and I had our own room at the foot of the stairs along with our own bathroom in the hall.

Violet prayed for love and happiness. She would pray daily that God would meet her needs.

Psalm 61:3
    For you have been my refuge, a strong tower against the foe.

Discipline

The family was given very strict household rules. Plastic was placed on the new carpet all through the house up and down the stairs so it wouldn't get dirty. We all removed our shoes at the door. We had strict rules about the living room. No one was allowed to sit in the living room unless they were playing the piano or the family had company. The TV was not on unless chores were completed. Each one of us had to do the dishes and clean the kitchen. We spent a lot of time around the kitchen table, doing homework or sitting up in our rooms playing games. Mom loved to cook and we all cleaned up after her messy eventful dinners. Everything would be quiet until Kyle came home from work. He asked questions about everything, the mail, something new on the kitchen counter, who was Mom talking to on the phone and checked out everything that had happened while he was at work. He would yell up the stairs and make us come downstairs and give a report as to what we had done and if our dirty underclothes were placed in the hamper downstairs. He never picked on me or Janice. Mom told Kyle straight up, "You can strike your children's legs, but Linda and Janice are mine and I'll take care of them." I remember that most of the time his kids were punished because of dirty clothes being on the floor of their bedrooms. Sometimes they were stuffed in the drawers or closets, and boy, that action was grounds for major punishment. As I look back I see that he picked on them to show Mom that he could have some control over something. He only had an eighth grade education and his English was very poor. He couldn't control Mom or us so he controlled his children.

Psalm 86:6-7
Hear my prayer, O Lord. Listen to my cry for mercy. In the day of my trouble I will call to You, for You will answer me.

Moving the Business

Two years later it was time to look for a new daycare close to home. Mom had grown the business and now needed to find more space. She sold the property on Hale Street and used it as a down payment on a house located on Dixie Highway across the street from our home. It had to be licensed by the state and up to code. All new rules and regulations were now in process. Mom joined the LACUS (Louisville Association of Children under Six) group and got involved with the process of regulating the standards for private daycare. She was eventually asked to be president of the local group. Her new daycare was painted and decorated to be child friendly. It had a small office in the front room and rooms for babies, toddlers, preschool children and after school children. New toys were purchased to fit the needs of each age group. She made her own cots that could be folded up and stacked neatly away. She cooked all the lunches and did all the grocery shopping. She still had to transport school children to three different schools. It was a model daycare for other people who were preschool educators. She was asked to teach classes for the state. Many preschool educators came to observe her method of teaching and arranging of a private nursery school. She protected the children from outside strangers by using a public address system. The children would come to the office when their name was called to meet the parent for dismissal. It was very organized.

As the enrollment increased so did her employees. She had regular meetings with all of her employees. Her main focus was that each employee cared for the children as if they were her own children. She served lunch family style so each child would get as much food as they wanted. She also wanted the employees to know that food should not be wasted. Her employees were treated like family, but she ran a tight ship. She allowed them to eat lunch free and take breaks when needed. All of her employees from the old daycare came with her to her new place. Most of her children also followed. Some of her employees stayed for over twenty-five years. She had a way of loving each person she met. She would bring fresh tomatoes to employees and fix special dishes for them for lunch. She liked to joke around with them, yet they knew that when she was mad about something that was wrong she would address it right away. She didn't care if she hurt your feelings. She would correct the problem, and later explain why she was upset and wanted the problem corrected. She had no problem firing employees that were not faithful to the business or those who were not doing their job. She was a tough woman to figure out, but you always knew that she was fair. I have seen her pray about situations before she returned to work to correct problems.

She had a personal relationship with each one of her parents. She was often a listening ear for mothers who were going through divorce. The love of God never left her heart. She took every opportunity to witness to everyone about her faith. She invited non-Christians to attend her church. She prayed with worried women who were in abusive situations. She loaned money to people she didn't really know. Parents who confided in her that they had no food and no way to pay her for childcare were given a special payment plan. She opened her daycare for mothers who had to work during snow storms. I remember once she kept a small boy for three days while his single mother worked in a hospital downtown.

Kyle was always present in each part of her business. He went on day work and this was a blessing for her. She could do what she wanted and only had to deal with his control issues at night. After a long day at the nursery she still had to come home and cook for a family of six. Janice would start supper for her and she would finish it when she came home. Kyle and the rest of us would do dishes with him controlling our every movement. I remember one night we all got into an argument about who didn't do what. It led to my kids and your kids and money. Mom was so sick of him she told me to get my clothes and we were leaving. She left him and we went to the nursery and slept upstairs in the unfinished attic so she could open the nursery at 6:00 the next morning. We slept on the floor. I remember being very upset and worried about what would happen to our home. Again we were all upset. This argument went on for weeks. I was hoping that they would get a divorce and just leave us all alone. Kyle soon told her he was sorry and they went back together.

Violet had been through one divorce. She had prayed for a Godly man and she felt that Kyle was the answer to her prayer. Her relationship with Christ had strengthened and she felt that it was God's will for her to be obedient to her new husband.

She trusted in God to supply her needs and she felt that she needed Kyle.

Proverbs 3:5

Trust in the Lord with all thine heart; and lean not unto thine own understanding.

The Business Grows

Mom was never happy. She put her whole body and soul into her business. They got permission to build on to the back of the house and make space for more children. She now had seventy-five children. She started a kindergarten and hired a certified kindergarten teacher to teach the class. Her job as director extended to working overtime cleaning and mopping floors. Each weekend she would take home all the sheets and blankets from each child so they would be clean on Monday for the next week. We didn't have a clothes dryer. She would wash over 70 sheets and have each one of us hang the sheets outside or downstairs on the lines in the basement. We hated week-ends and laundry.

Violet wore many hats. She was the bookkeeper, cook, bus driver, janitor, and mother of four. She had to depend on all of the children to work around the house. We learned to iron and clean. Bessie had been a good example for Violet. She was not afraid of hard work and she expected each one of her children to work along with her.

Violet listed work at the top of her list of judging the importance of a person. She had no use for a lazy person.

2 Thessalonians 3:10-11

For even when we were with you, we gave you this rule: "If a man will not work, he shall not eat." We hear that some of you are idle. They are not busy; they are busybodies.

Visitation

Daddy was now married and had two children. We could only see our father on week-ends. He was also a lonely person. He was still drinking and his new wife was not happy with his lack of devotion to her family. He got fired from his jobs and was also picked up for drinking and driving. He loved us girls and we looked forward to being with him.

Whenever he would call us, my mother would stand by the phone and listen to our conversations. She would tell us to tell him we needed new shoes. Tell him you need money for school. Tell him he needs to send you money. I always felt like I was never able to talk to him about anything. He would try to talk to us, but mom would be on the other end of the phone telling us what to say. It was rough trying to have a relationship with my father when my mother would monitor everything I said. Her anger would always pour out into our relationship with Daddy. When he would pick us up to spend time with him we could not go anywhere. He would have to take us for rides around town or to a park to play ball. He loved to go down to the river and park and watch the boats come in. He loved to play ball and pitch ball with Janice. Daddy was always loving toward us. He never forgot to bring us gifts for Easter, Christmas, and always helped me pick out a pumpkin for Halloween. His pet name for me was Pumpkin. He called my sister "Sissy" or "Janny Kaysis." He was funny and liked to sing with us in the car. He never said anything bad about my mother. As time went on, he began to get depressed. He got a job at the hardware store in Shively where we lived. Mom would take me up there to get rabbit food just to see him. Mom was still in love with him and he was still in love with her. She confessed on her death-bed that she had never stopped loving him.

One night while Janice was staying with mom at the hospital, Mom confessed that Daddy came over to our house and told her he missed her something awful. He was passionately looking into her eyes and while they were both trying to figure out how things had gotten this far, Daddy grabbed Mom, pulled her over on the couch and made love to her. He said, "You don't know how much I have missed you." She wanted to say the same back to him. Instead Mom asked him to leave and she never saw him again. I am sure she relived that day over and over in her mind.

Maybe this is why she thought she had to marry Kyle.

Daddy never caught up with his child support. His life at home with his new children was not going well. His new wife had asked for a divorce. He started drinking so bad that he couldn't hold down a job. He was fired from an elevator company where he was making good money.

One night he called us and wanted to talk to my sister Janice. She was now in college and on her own at Georgetown University. He was drunk and wanted to talk to her about his life. He was hungry and she made him some tomato soup. He also asked her if she could bring him a pair of shoes. It was so sad. He was all alone and needed to get his life back together. Janice went with my uncle to meet him at his home. He was very sick and couldn't breathe. He needed to be in the hospital, but did not want to go. He told her he loved us and that he was sorry and wished things were different. He should have been admitted to a rehab center that night. At Christmas he came to get us and give us gifts. He was so drunk that my sister's boyfriend followed us to make sure we were all right. He ran into my sister's parked car and didn't even know it. He cried the whole time he was with us. It was so upsetting to me. Janice drove him home and then we rode home with the boyfriend. I know we saw him once more before January but he was still out of work and separated from his family.

Proverbs 14:14
   The faithless will be fully repaid for their ways, and the good man rewarded for his ways.

The Tragic End

In January of 1966, my father's twin brother Ira died of a heart attack. This was the last straw for Ora. I remember going to the funeral home to see his brother, and he took us back to the break room and talked to us. He loved us and hugged us a lot. He did not want us to leave him. I remember a little girl came and asked him for a dime for a coke. It was his daughter Sally. It was the first time I had ever seen him with another child. He didn't stop to talk to her or tell us who she was, but gave her a dime and hurried her on to the coke machine. It was as if she never existed.

Daddy went back with his wife, but never stopped drinking. In March of 1967 he got very, very sick. The alcohol had taken over his body. I only saw him when my sister came home from school. My mom would tell me that he didn't want us. She would punish me by saying, "I am going to call your daddy and you can just go live with him and his mean wife." I was always afraid that no one really wanted me. I felt guilty if I misbehaved and would cry and plead for forgiveness.

The last time I saw him he was in the hospital and was in intensive care. His sister called us and told us that he was sick and we needed to come and see him in the hospital. When Janice got home on Friday, we went straight to the hospital and sat with all his family. I had never been around his family. I was quiet and felt out of place. Mom said that they divorced us when the family split. I really think it was mom who kept us from seeing them. His wife was in the room with him. We waited for her to leave so we could go in and see him. I remember he was on oxygen and weak. He was very happy to see us. Janice kissed him first and then he looked at me and said there's my pumpkin. He said "I am very sick. I am having trouble breathing." I had never seen him look that way. He had lost weight and was not shaved. He didn't have his glasses on and had lost control of his bowls. His hair was totally gray. He told Janice something about mom and she didn't really seem to understand what he was trying to say. He wanted to hold on to us and kissed us good-by. He cried the whole time we were there. We told him we would come back to see him next weekend and left the room. The family said they would keep in touch with us as we walked out to the elevator.

The next week Janice came home from school early and told Mom she wanted to go to the hospital. Mom started to cry, "Your father is gone. He died this morning." She was so upset.

"Did you tell Linda?" asked Janice.

"No," replied Mom. "She has a spring concert at school tonight and it's a big deal to her. I bought her a new long dress and she has been looking forward to this for a long time. There's no need to upset her right now. I'll tell her later after the concert."

We ate supper as usual and Janice's boyfriend, Leroy, was there to eat with us. I remember getting ready for the choir concert and coming down the stairs to get approval from the family. Everyone looked like they were crying and they were not really interested in what I looked like. I remember that Leroy took me to school. I thought that was strange. Usually Mom, Kyle or Janice would have taken me. I knew something was wrong, but I didn't want to think about it. I hoped they would show up at the concert. I remember looking for them as soon as we were placed on the risers. They came in late, but they were there. We sang our songs and the choir had pictures taken by parents. Mom didn't take any pictures. We hurried out and got into the car. Kyle wasn't there. Mom and Janice took me home. I remember waiting in line to get out of the parking lot of the school. Janice started crying and Mom told me that Daddy was gone. It was a quiet ride home. Daddy died on Good Friday. The next day we found out that his casket would be open for viewing on Saturday afternoon and Sunday (Easter). He was then buried on Monday. We also learned that the funeral home had the doors locked unless his wife was there. She wanted to make sure that our family members, especially my mom, would not be able to visit without her being present.

On Saturday afternoon we went to the funeral home. It was hard to see him just lying there. His wife came over and stood beside me. I don't think I even looked at her. My aunt and uncle came with us just for support. My cousin Wilma who had lived with Mom and Daddy sat with us and made us feel welcomed. She told us how much she loved me when I was just a baby. Janice connected with other cousins and family from the country. I remember I felt numb. His children were not at the funeral. I don't know if they were ever taken there before the people came for viewing, but we never saw them. At the funeral all the family was seated up front. We were seated in the back. We were not acknowledged that we were family. At the grave-side I remember crying very hard and someone trying to comfort me. The funeral director would not allow us to sit down because he said it was for the family. My sister and I were so hurt. We were always driven away from our father by our mother. Now at his funeral, we were told that we were not family. I wondered, "Who is our family?"

I remember going home and finding my Easter basket Mom made. It meant nothing to me now. I sat there staring out the big front window in the living room of our house. I wanted to grieve but didn't want my mom to see me. Somehow I needed to find a time when everyone was gone and review the past few days in my mind. "Why couldn't we have had the home I had always wished for? Is this what a family was supposed to be like?" I was miserable! I had a lot to say but couldn't.

The gospel of Mark tells us that Jesus knew that he was going to be sacrificed for our sins. I wonder if he ever wished he had said more to his disciples.

I believed that Jesus grieved. Not for himself but for his disciples. I only wish I had been more mature in the gospel. I would have been able to understand that when we are born again in Jesus we will not fear death but will look forward to everlasting life in heaven with Jesus Christ our Savior.

Mark 14:35
Going a little farther, He fell to the ground and prayed that if possible the hour might pass from Him.

Pressing Forward

I knew for sure that Kyle was not my family. I detested everything he did. Mom would push us on him. Ask him to take us to piano lessons and get things at the store for us. She wanted to make us one big happy family. He always did what she wanted, but I wasn't happy. I was now thirteen years old. I had been punished several times by my mom who threatened to send me to live with my dad and his new wife. I was a shy child, not really bucking the establishment. I mostly got into trouble for not practicing the piano and speaking what was on my mind. Now she had to find some other form of punishment. I was angry with her. She was becoming just like Kyle controlling and unsympathetic of my emotional feelings.

Unsympathetic is a good word for Mom. She never knew how to just be a mom. All I wanted to do was tell her how I felt about things. When we got too emotional, she would say, "Oh, you kids should have grown up like we did. You were born with a silver spoon in your mouth." We never got to share any problems that concerned us. I longed for her to hold me in her lap and let me tell her about my inner feelings. I couldn't say anything negative about Sarah, Ron or Kyle. This was surely a touchy subject.

She didn't get involved with anything I was doing at school. My grades were failing and she would yell at me and tell me she wished that I was smart like Ron. She would have Ron give me spelling words and help me with math. He would call me dumb and laugh at me. Can you imagine how hard it was for me to deal with family matters and school? I was placed in a slower math class and I doubt my mom ever knew it. I would hide my report card and once changed the grade so I wouldn't get laughed at by the other kids. I became very angry. Some of my anger came from diet pills. When I was in the third grade Mom took me to a diet doctor who gave me diet pills. I remember they would not allow me to sleep. She was also taking pills. This allowed her to work from morning till night. It only made me nervous and angry. I would play with my hair a lot and became compulsive in some of my actions.

She was always comparing me to Sarah and Ron. They do everything their daddy tells them to do. They never talk back or voice their opinion. I wanted to say, "Yes and they know better than to move unless he commands them to do so." When she couldn't threaten to send me to Daddy, she would threaten me with Kyle. "I should let Kyle get a hold of you and he would straighten you out." I remember spending a lot of time in my room when I didn't want to see any of the family.

Violet had grown up without a realization of her true identity. She lived her life around the acceptance of others. Her sense of self-worth was never shaped by her parents, or, either of her husband's. She never saw the value in praising her children. Mom disciplined with negative comments. We experienced deep wounds, mild emotional abrasions and verbal abuse. It was important that we conform to her expectations. In return we learned to do anything to please Mom and other people in our lives.

Proverbs 23:7
As a man thinks within himself, so he is.

Christ is the Answer

Violet was always true to her belief in God. She took on offices at church and spent time in prayer for anyone who was in need. Her belief in God was so important to her as a mother. She would always tell her children that Church came first. The family went to church every Sunday, no questions asked. Each member had to be dressed up and hair was of most importance. Every Saturday night she would wash all three girl's hair. Then she would pin curl the hair with bobby pins. They would sleep on the pins and the next morning each had curls going everywhere. Each girl took turns sitting between her knees on their knees handing her bobby pins as she twisted little bits of hair through her fingers. She loved to watch "Lawrence Welk." She twisted hair while she watched her favorite show. I remember that this ritual took place until I was eleven or twelve years old. I hated the hair thing. We all did. She wanted to put on a big show at church. Everyone thought we were the perfect family as we rolled into the church parking lot in the old station wagon. This was the happiest time of her life. She loved to show off the family.

Mom loved the preachers' families. She would invite them to lunch on Sundays. She would give them things when she started making a little money in her business. She canned food and would share this with their families. She gave them money to buy things they needed. Once she bought a TV for our preacher who only had a black and white little TV. She loved the preacher's kids and volunteered to babysit them when necessary. I remember that we once kept a minister's baby for a week so they could take a trip to Florida.

She paid to have a new baptism pool installed in the Methodist church. She felt that everyone should have the choice of being immersed or sprinkled. She paid for a tent rental for a huge tent revival that brought in crowds of people to be saved. She gave a seed faith to a minister so he could start a school and a scholarship fund for young ministers. I recently received a letter from our old minister who held the tent revival. After all these years, the school was growing and our minister friend's son, who is also a minister, received the scholarship for 2007. She would have been so proud. Her money is still growing.

She also housed singers and groups of people when we had guests on Sunday mornings. She enjoyed hosting dinners in our home for special evangelist and ministers at our church. She invited ministers to the lake to go fish and became more than just friends with each one. Her mission in life was to take care of the pastor and his family. Each Christmas you can bet she would have a Christmas dinner for the minister's family, along with other special people in the church. Mom always made homemade pies and spent all day in the kitchen cooking up everything from fresh corn to her unique chicken and dumplings. The dirty dishes were left for us girls along with the babysitting of the minister's children while they entertained guests in the living room. After dinner she would have Janice and Ron play the piano and organ and sing for the guests. She was so proud of Janice. She would always have her sing for everyone. Eventually the evening would end with a group singing favorite hymns around the piano. In those brief moments Violet finally had the perfect family she had dreamed about. She loved her home and she loved showing it off to others. Little did they know that a storm was always brewing inside that fake loving family.

I cannot begin to list all the things that she did for ministers and the church. She felt that God was so good to her and she had to do her best to give back to him and to the church. I sometimes believed that she thought that you had to earn your way into heaven. If this is true (and I have since learned that it is not), she certainly must have a seat in heaven next to all the high saints. Isn't it sad? After all those years she had it all wrong.

I don't think my grandfather believed in works. I found an article he wrote that says, "You must be born again, it's the only way to get to heaven."

I do appreciate that she thought she was setting examples by making the family watch religious programs on TV. Every time Billy Graham would come on TV, she would make us stop what we were doing and come watch him. We could not take a call on the phone, read a book or even speak a word when he was on. We had to sit there until the last *Just as I Am* was sung and the people were all standing in front of the stadium.

Mom would read her Bible, but she didn't have real knowledge of what it was teaching. She quoted what she wanted to quote. She was strict with the rules set for all of us. We had to report to her on every event that took place in our lives, especially when we started going out with friends. We only went with church friends and dated church friends. We had to be home by 11:00 and after high school it was extended to 12:00. It remained 12:00 even after I turned twenty-one and lived at home until I turned twenty-seven years old. She never allowed us to dance or play cards. Our skirts had to be below the knee and our tops and sweaters had to be conservative. Our swim suits were one piece or showed little midriff area. Every piece of clothing had to be checked out by her before the tags were removed.

We never had any kind of liquor in the house or any kind of smoking. We did not cuss or talk back to adults. God was always judging our actions and she let us know that we were being judged. She made it sound like God was always sitting up there with a chalk board keeping score when we misbehaved. I became afraid to sin. Somehow she always knew when I would try to lie to her or let things slide not telling the whole truth. I was always praying for forgiveness. Somehow I knew that God was going to get me. Like my mother, I lived a guilt-ridden life. I too longed for a perfect Christian family. We both were looking for love.

While writing her story she made it clear that God was her business partner and she depended on prayer for her daily life. When I think of the things she went through with each of her marriages I realize that only her faith in God could have kept her going. She did not love herself and therefore, she looked to God and religion for affirmation.

Psalm 145:14-16

> *The Lord sustains all who fall, and raises up all who are bowed down. The eyes of all look to Thee, and Thou dost give them their food in due time. Thou dost open Thy hand, and dost satisfy the desire of every living thing.*

Success in the Sixties

Violet was a self made woman. Her success in life was amazing. In the early sixties, she was featured twice in the Sunday newspaper. It displayed pictures of her daycare and the learning experiences that were available for children in her school. She loved nature and believed that children learned by experiencing and exploring on their own. She placed two fish tanks in the office to keep the kids calm, distracted and involved as the parents slipped away to go off to work. Her love of animals was shared by hatching chicks and ducks in the spring. She built a duck pond in the back yard and a chicken coop next to the duck pond so the children could gather eggs in the mornings. They also participated in cleaning out the duck pond in the summer and feeding the animals. She bought a pet lamb that was bottle fed along with rabbits that were placed in a fenced in area for observing. Petting the tame rabbits was therapeutic for shy children. The outdoor environment gave opportunities for developing language skills and provided stories for creative story time. A figure eight was made in the middle of the yard so small tricycles could pass by fake traffic signs pretending that they were traveling on a real road. Walking boards and jungle gyms were provided for large muscle development.

The children were given opportunities daily to experience outdoor play. When she purchased the building next door she had lots of room for swings and even a trampoline. Employees were not allowed to sit down on the playground. She encouraged them to get involved with the play and make sure that everyone was involved and safe.

Mom was happiest when she was in her business and working to make it a bigger and happier place for children. She was certainly ahead of her time when it came to teaching children hands on activities. Inside she made clay from water, flower, salt and food coloring. Children painted on tables wrapped in butcher paper. She hired a very creative kindergarten teacher who had taught in Japan. She brought many new experiences to the business. Her creative ideas were shared with the staff. Kindergarten was not mandatory in the public schools. She had one of the most creative kindergartens in town. She had little graduation ceremonies and invited parents and grandparents.

The late sixties and early seventies brought on new rules and regulations for education. Private kindergartens were not acknowledged as certified in the local school system. She joined other private daycares and formed an organization that allowed owners to have a voice in Frankfort for education. She lobbied in Frankfort for children's rights and working mother's rights. New rules and regulations made it almost impossible to run a private daycare. Inspectors were sent all over the state requiring owners to buy and install certain types of doors, flooring and other equipment that was not affordable to the long time owners. The outdoor animals were taken out and the playground was changed to meet all the new rules. The most frustrating thing was the rules would change with each inspection. Wanting to follow the state rules and stay in business, the private daycares wrote letters and went to Frankfort demanding they receive in writing what was expected of each center. Most of the women who were inspecting the centers had not even worked in child care. Mom became a part time lobbyist in Frankfort.

In her daily journal she writes,

House bill 79 and 643 was voted on Thursday in the senate. All of our hard work helped. The bill passed 37-1. We are so happy! Now we have to see what Governor Carroll does.

Her biggest beef was unlicensed homes keeping children without the knowledge of the state regulations. She was asked to sit down with preschool educators from Louisville and list needs and safety rules that would pertain to private daycares. Her record in Frankfort was very impressive. Many references were made to her when a discussion of private daycare came before the many law makers who worked with preschool establishments. She taught classes for the state and told how she started her business giving important facts that would challenge young owners to make children a priority in their business. It was an honor to teach along side of her in 1977 in an early childhood convention held in Louisville. I was a graduate student from University of Louisville talking about the ages and stages of development and she was in the next classroom teaching about building a business that works. Centers from all over Kentucky and surrounding states were attending for credited hours. My professor from University Of Louisville knew of my mother. She was impressed with her accomplishments in the '50s and '60s and made a special trip to her center to visit. By now she was known all over Louisville as Miss Violet, the owner of the little pink school on Dixie. Everyone knew her and many wanted to meet her. She certainly had the formula for making her business a success. This gave her the happiness she needed.

We all make the wrong assumption that, "I must meet certain standers of success in order to feel good about myself." Violet had this mindset. She passed it down to each of us girls. This trap of being a perfectionist caused severe challenges in our lives.

We should not submit to the commandments and teachings of men. They have no value.

Colossians 2:20-23

Since you died with Christ to the elemental spiritual forces of this world, why, as though you still belonged to the world, do you submit to its rules: "Do not handle! Do not taste! Do not touch!"? These rules, which have to do with things that are all destined to perish with use, are based on merely human commands and teachings. Such regulations indeed have an appearance of wisdom, with their self-imposed worship, their false humility and their harsh treatment of the body, but they lack any value in restraining sensual indulgence.

Adding Buildings to the Business

In the early '70s Mom had 120 children attending her school and she had to build on under the new addition. By 1975, Violet had bought the house next door and added an arch way to connect to the existing building. In 1978, she was looking for more space and bought the building one house away from the nursery to make room for all the kindergarten children. The private kindergarten class, which had grown to forty children and two full time teachers, had a waiting list. In her journal she writes. *September 30th, 1978 I took $12,000.00 to the dentist office down the street and got the keys to open the building and start my new kindergarten.* She was licensed to have 185 children and was about to meet her quota with 161. Her prices were now $50 per week for one child.

Violet lost her mother, Bessie, in 1962. Her father came to her house to stay for awhile and returned home to pastor yet another new church. At this time in Violet's life she had no one to help with housekeeping. She became very dependent on all of us to clean house. Mom was so uptight about everything. She was over worked and stressed. We became like little slaves, being punished when things were not done to her specification.

I can remember being punished for leaving strawberries in the sink all afternoon. I had seen her wash them and I thought you soaked them before you steamed them. She didn't give us instructions. We ruined a whole gallon of berries. Her depression from her mother's death and a steady diet of reducing pills kept her totally involved in building her business. Kyle was now on second shift, leaving home at 2:00 in the afternoon and returning at 11:30 at night. Having him there in her face at the business was a mixed blessing. He could go get groceries, but he would spend all of his free time nosing around in the daycare acting like a fix-it man.

Mom hired her little sister to work for her. She would keep an eye on Kyle. Teen would tell her how Kyle would freely get money out of the cash register whenever he needed something. He also liked to flirt with the employees. Mom didn't want to believe anything bad about him. We always thought she was naïve until she placed my name and my sister's name on the deeds to each of her new buildings. Kyle wasn't even aware of the business part. He didn't even know how to write a check. It was her wishes that Janice and I would take over the business when she retired. She made this very clear almost on a daily basis.

We both grew up in the business and worked in it most of our lives. Every summer I watched kids, told stories, sang songs, ran errands and gave breaks during naptime. I had been changing diapers since I was six years old. I knew every aspect of the daycare. After school I would go back to work with Mom and remain there until she closed for the evening.

I remember once when I was very small a young baby stayed with us for a few days. I asked my sister about it and she told me the story. A young mother stopped by the nursery and laid her week-old baby on the bed. She told my Mom, "You have to help me." She had delivered this baby while her husband was in the service and now he was returning home. She couldn't let her husband know that she had cheated on him. She needed a good home for the baby. Mom listened to her story and took the baby. She called my grandfather in Indiana and asked if he knew of a young couple who wanted to adopt a baby. It just so happened, that he had the perfect couple who had prayed for children but could not have any of their own. Mom took the baby to the young couple and the baby was never aware that he was adopted. This all took place in the '50s when social workers were not easy to contact. Mom never told anyone about the baby and the paper work was never traced to Kentucky.

In the early '70s a child was left at the daycare for a weekend. We tried to call all the emergency numbers and could not find one person at home. Mom hated to call the police so she took care of him, bought him some clothes, took him to church and on Monday his mother called in a panic. There was a big misunderstanding between the mother and father who were separated. The mother thought the father had the child and the father didn't know that it was his weekend to have the child. Each parent had gone out of town and the grandparents were also away from home. The child had a wonderful time at our house. We played games with him and gave him more attention than he would have had at either home.

Mark 9:37
Whoever welcomes one of these little children in My name welcomes Me.

Growing a Business
and Raising a Family

In our house it was a sin to spend time sitting or sleeping. You must be productive. After Janice left home for college, Mom separated the three of us, Ron, Sarah, and me, so we could work and not fight over chores. I was assigned to daycare after school. They had house chores like dusting and sweeping. I am not sure who had the best job. I do know that I spent all of my summers watching kids. Mom always said she was glad she had girls, but she seemed to make a difference between us girls and Ron. He really had her fooled. In her eyes he could do no wrong. This was not the case. Looking back, I remember there was the time he went to church and told everyone that we won a trip to Disney World from a contest on the back of a box of cereal. Everyone was congratulating us and mom felt like a fool. I remember Kyle punished him and made him stay in his room all day for that lie. Mom made him go back to church the next Sunday and tell the teachers and class that he lied. He loved the attention.

We all needed counseling. There was so much tension in our family. We were always afraid we were not going to please our parents.

Every one of us was mentally abused. Mom was stepping into the mold of Kyle's negative attitudes. They looked for things to go wrong. Even little problems were made into big deals. Mom was always a nervous wreck. When we were not working, we were worthless. When our grades were bad, we were dumb. When we gained weight, we were fat. When we made mistakes, we were stupid. When our hair was not combed to perfection, we were ugly. Being a child in that house earned the lowest form of self-esteem that one could acquire.

Kyle took control of everything. Her employees were even

afraid of him. He took every opportunity to tell them how to place lids on garbage cans, park their cars and clean out cabinets. He strutted around the property like a rooster in a hen house. Most of the staff, who had been with Mom for years, just made fun of him and learned to ignore his bossy behavior. They hated to see him come in the door and took everything he said in stride. They were so dedicated to Mom that they would never go to her and tell her what he was doing. My aunt was very much aware of his presents. She would share things with us girls and knew she could never rock the boat with Mom. Teen learned from experience to keep her mouth shut.

In 1970, Ron graduated from school, Sarah got married and left town and Janice was married and teaching school. I was still in high school. I hated being home with them fighting all the time. Kyle was always around during the day, and at night Mom and I would work at the nursery and find us something to eat around 6:00 at night. The stress of the business was changing her. I remember one day during the summer, mom needed someone to work in the office while she was gone. I went into the office to work, and it offended one of the girls who thought she was in charge. This particular morning, this employee was responsible for a group of four-year-olds. I took over the office and answered the phone and did as I usually did every afternoon. The girl didn't like me being in charge. We had some words, but it wasn't a major problem. After lunch, this teacher didn't come back to work.

Mom thought I had offended her and she went into this huge rage. No one could calm her down. She wouldn't even listen to me or other employees that heard what had happened. It wasn't that big of a deal. It was a Friday afternoon, and then she cried all day long Saturday and on Sunday she made me go over to the girl's house and apologize to her for nothing. I couldn't believe that she wouldn't listen to me and take my side. After all, I was just doing what she told me to do. She said I wasn't as smart as this girl and didn't know how to deal with people. I had pure hell all weekend. I drove around town all day on Sunday and finally went to her apartment to say that I was sorry." She wasn't there. I wrote her a note and left it on the door. When Monday came I was so worn out with the situation and so was Mom. She was barely speaking to me. Kyle was bad mouthing me and making things worse. He told

Mom that she might be trying to get a job down the street. Mom went off again. She thought of everything bad. In fact, bad went to worse. I was a bad person and she told all the family what I had done. Monday morning rolled around and the employee came back. She had no intentions of leaving. She replied, "Remember I was supposed to take off early Friday to go to King's Island. It's no big deal."

This is just a minor situation compared to all the drama we went through all our lives. The daycare became the explosive dynamite that was used to blow up issues in the family. Kyle was so jealous of us girls. I was eighteen years old and a senior in high school when Kyle decided it was time he took charge of me. I was getting ready to go to school and Mom yelled up the stairs and asked me to do something for her. I don't really remember what it was, but I had an excuse for not doing what she wanted. I gave her a reason and she said I talked back to her. I don't remember what it was but I do remember what came next. She came rushing up the stairs and said, "Sarah and Ron would never talk to me that way."

I replied, "I am not Sarah and Ron. You think they are such angels. They're not! I am sick and tired of being compared to Sarah and Ron. You don't see them hanging around here, do you? They're glad to be out of this place."

She started to swing at me and I moved. You must remember Mom was on diet pills and very tired and angry at the world. By this time Kyle was on the steps. He grabbed me and pulled me down on the floor. I had a skirt on. He pulled me across his lap and started beating me.

He said, "I'll give you what you need." Mom just stood there saying I should have let him control you all these years. You wouldn't have had such a smart mouth. This was not the mother I knew. I bit Kyle and kicked him as hard as I could to get him off of me. He was really getting into the beating thing. I scratch his face and he continued to bruise me on the legs, arms and backside hitting me with all his angry might. My skirt was up over my head and I was totally humiliated. One swift kick and I got away and ran for the bathroom. I locked myself in the bathroom and tried to cut my wrist with a razor. It bled but I didn't have the nerve to continue the job. I just wanted to get out of there. I didn't make it to school that day. I packed my clothes and left home in my car. I drove around town and had nowhere to go. I came home when I knew Kyle had gone to work and Mom had gone to the daycare.

I had no money. I never got paid for any of the work I did at the daycare; although; she would give us money for just about anything we needed. She made sure we had to come to her to ask for money. She would never let us get a job away from the daycare. When she knew she was wrong she could never say she was sorry. Instead she would put a new sweater on your bed or buy you something that you wanted. We talked very little the next few days but she made it clear that her main concern after this confrontation was "What will Kyle's mom say if she sees **him**? She'll think you're a little monster." It didn't concern her that I was upset and tried to kill myself. I know now that I needed professional help. I needed away from home.

Violet had been through too much with the business and Kyle. Now she was trying to control every aspect of our lives. The pills were taking over her personality. She was not herself. It was the only thing that gave her the energy to keep up with her busy lifestyle. She had no idea that she was on speed. It was not illegal or questioned in the early '70s.

Mom's doctor gave her the pills to lose weight. She was always concerned about weight.

According to the following scripture, parents are supposed to give love, compassion, protection, provision, and loving discipline. I was beginning to lose heart! I longed for her love. I needed her to listen and understand.

Colossians 3:21
   Fathers, do not exasperate your children, that they may not lose heart.

Violet Needed Love

Mom hated Kyle's mom because his mother didn't respect us. Mom was always trying to impress her with her cooking and her money. Nothing ever worked. Kyle's mother hated my mom. She would visit all the family except ours. When she came over she would sit in the drive and honk the horn and mom would go out to see her. She would make excuses that she was not dressed up to come in or that her hair looked bad or she was in a hurry. His parents were very odd people full of hate and jealousy. She once told mom at a family dinner that she could never love her. This was such a blow to mom, especially, after she had done so much to try to gain her approval. Mom really needed love and acceptance from everyone she met.

After I graduated from high school, I wanted to go away to college. Mom was very much insistent that I stay at home and attend nursing school. I wanted away from home and the nursery. I wanted on my own. I applied to nursing schools all over Kentucky and was accepted by Jefferson Community School of Nursing located right down town. I agreed to stay at home, when I met a guy at church who I started dating. He too was going to attend the community college. When he was drafted into the army, I quit nursing school and I didn't really care what I did. My mom was very upset with me. She demanded that I attend college.

I knew that I was good at teaching children, so I applied to the school of education at University of Louisville. I was immediately accepted and started my career as an elementary school teacher. Mom was now happy again. She was paying for my education and I had no choice but to do as she wished. In some crazy, dumb way I was always trying to please her. I wanted so much to get the love I deserved. She often told me she loved me and that I was pretty, but in the next breath she would tear me down concerning my weight or my hair. I realized that she loved me so much that she wanted me to be perfect. Of course I would like to say that I was perfect, but I am far from it.

I was determining my self-worth by the praise and love that my mother was giving me. It wasn't until years later that I would learn that God is my guide and judge.

Colossians 2:10
And in Him you have been made complete, and He is the head over all rule and authority.

Facing New Changes in Life

In 1970, Mom became a grandmother. She was so excited about her new role in life. We all wanted a little girl, but our little boy became the love of her life. My sister gave birth to a son whom she freely shared with Mom and me. She was teaching school and going to graduate school after work. Her husband was also attending graduate school and going to the National Guard after work. The baby went to day care in the mornings and I would pick him up in the afternoons and take him home with me for his nap. Mom's whole personality seemed to change at this time. She took some time away from work to take CT to the park and on special rides to get strawberries and mushrooms. She started going to the lake with my aunt and uncle. Although you could never be too far away from the daycare, it did seem that she was beginning to relax some. She now had something to live for again. Little did she realize that she would soon be responsible for her aging father and babysitting would take on a new meaning.

My grandfather side swiped a car on a highway on his trip to Louisville. We got a phone call about 8:00 at night from the Indiana state trooper and said that he was holding him for a hit and run. Mom and I called my aunt and uncle and headed toward a little town of Edwardsville, Indiana. My grandfather, Ona, was now in his early seventies and his new wife was just a little bit younger. They had no idea that they had hit anything. Mom and I exchanged insurance cards, and she drove his car home while I drove our car home. Little did she know that this accident was going to be the next tragic event to take place in her dysfunctional home.

My aunt and Mom spent the next few days trying to tell my grandfather that he was no longer able to drive his car. He was a tough nut to crack. He refused to listen to them and said they were ganging up on him. He had an appointment with the doctor the next day, and the doctor told the family that he was getting hardening of the arteries. Now we call it Alzheimer's. He gave him blood thinners and we took him home to Indiana without his car. My aunt in Indiana would check up on them each weekend. It wasn't long until they were totally unable to stay by themselves and make rational decisions. Bills hadn't been paid and old food was in the refrigerator. One Sunday my aunt made a surprise visit only to find a street person sleeping on my grandfather's couch.

"Daddy, who's the man sleeping on the couch?"

Ona looked her right in the face and said, "I have no idea."

His clothes were all torn and he looked like he hadn't bathed or shaved in months. He reeked of alcohol. "What do you mean you don't know?"

"Well," replied Ona, "he walked up on the steps and asked Ruth and I if we could help him find a place to sleep. He looked like he was down on his luck so we invited him in and he ate some food. Poor thing, I guess he just made himself at home right there on the couch."

Teen scolded him.

"Daddy, never ever do something like that again!"

Ona, got mad and said, "I can't believe you would get upset with me for helping out a poor old feller. He's not going to do anything to us."

"Yes," replied my aunt, "but you don't know that. Let's wake him up and send him on his way."

The man was certainly ready to run when he saw two new faces starring down at him. He jumped up, ran and never looked back.

Mom and her sisters had a long discussion about this event. They realized that my grandfather and his wife, Ruth, could not stay by themselves. Ruth was as bad as he was, if not worse. She had been a preacher's wife and knew my grandparents from church conference. When Ona learned that her husband had passed away he went to see her. It wasn't long until they were going back and forth to church together and got married.

Ruth had a mother that lived with them. She was one hundred and two years old, a nice looking woman who could care for herself and just enjoyed sitting in a chair watching TV or looking through picture books. She couldn't hear very well, but what she heard she understood. I remember visiting one summer and Ruth fixed my cousin and I lunch. It happened to be the day the astronauts walked on the moon. Ruth had the news on and was trying to get her mother to watch the men on the moon. You must know that Ruth was hard of hearing herself. She yelled at everyone and was use to yelling at her mother. She walked over to her mother with a loud voice and started screaming "Mother! The men are walking on the moon."

Her mother looked up at the television and quietly said, "That's nice dear!"

I just about rolled in the floor. She knew that Ruth wanted to show her something, but she didn't want to deal with her. She just kept reading her book as if she didn't exist. I know she yelled at her for at least ten minutes. Then her mother looked at me and shook her head as if to say, "Boy, is she crazy!"

By lunchtime I thought I had all the entertainment I needed, but there was more to come. Ruth lost her dusting spray called, "Jubilee." She kept saying over and over, "Have you seen my Jubilee?"

Her mother looked up at her and said, "You mean the gospel singers? Turn to another channel. They may be on channel five."

Ruth continued to try to explain about the space news, and her poor mother was just worn out with Ruth yelling. She looked her straight in the face and yelled, "Why don't you just sit down and watch the Jubilee singers?"

It wasn't long after Ruth's mother died that Ruth and my grandfather came to live with our family. Mom had full responsibility for them. She also was taking care of her grandbaby. Her life would change once again. She had all the responsibility of the business, she had to deal with Kyle, and now she had her father. I was still living at home going to college, and I helped her every spare minute I had. It was hard to study with the baby and the two senile seniors that were always trying to escape.

Mom called upon the Lord daily to give her strength.

Proverbs 3:5
   Trust in the Lord with all your heart and lean not on your own understanding.

Raising a Second Family

Ona and Ruth's behavior got more bizarre every day. As Mom would leave for work, she would give them breakfast and activities to do until she could check up on them at noon. There was a busy highway between our house and the nursery. Mom would look out the window and see them trying to cross the busy highway. They would often leave the house to take a walk and get lost.

Eventually, we had to stay with them twenty-four hours a day. In the summer, we took turns entertaining them with coloring books and even coloring in patterns on a tablecloth. Kyle would take Ona with him to run errands.

One time, he went into a store and Ona got out of the car and tried to approach an armored car. The guy with the money bag was trying to order him back with no success. Ona thought he recognized him. Kyle came out just in time. The guard had him backed up against the armored car so the man with the money could go into the store. I don't even think he realized that he did anything wrong.

Ona was always trying to witness to people about the Lord. He didn't like to see young people smoke and drink. He would walk up to people on the street and say "Shame on you for smoking that cigarette." We never knew what he was going to do. Ruth, on the other hand, started cussing. Her main phrase was, "G-D son of a bitch." She would also sing "Jingle Bells" over and over and over. She could also whistle it in tune with her buzzing hearing aids. Mom would take her to church on Sunday and she would sit there and get bored. Poor thing she could hardly hear. She would start singing "Jingle Bells," take her teeth out put them in her purse and snap the purse so everyone on the other side of the room could hear her. Then she would repeat "G-D son of a bitch" in between verses of "Jingle Bells." I sang in the choir and I could see and hear her. My Mom would take her purse away and she would scream,

"Son of a bitch." It got so bad that Mom didn't want them around any of her friends. When she would scold Ruth for cussing she would say, "Oh Violet, I didn't know I said that. Just smack me if I say it again." Five minutes later she would go right into her routine singing and cussing.

This was a hard time for Mom. Working all day long at the daycare, taking the two of them back and forth to the doctor's office and making sure they were safe and had food on the table. There was so much confusion going on in the house. To make matters worse, they would get up in the middle of the night and get dressed. Then they would turn the TV on really loud and sit in front of the test pattern.

I remember we would all wake up one at a time and sit at the top of the stairs watching them roam around the house. None of us could sleep. Ruth would do dishes at 3:00 in the morning. During the day they would want to take a walk. It was okay if we were walking behind them, but we had to keep the doors bolted and locked so they wouldn't roam outside at night.

Mom was so stressed out. Each day they would pack their suitcases and we would unpack their suitcases. They started to long to go home. Day after day they would ask to go home. I remember Mom and my aunt would try to reason with them. It was useless.

One Christmas Mom was fixing dinner for Kyle's family. The unhappy little couple had worn her out. Walking back and forth in and out of the kitchen packing and unpacking, singing and cussing. It was impossible for her to cook a meal for twenty-five people. She looked at me and said, "Take them for a ride."

I talked them into getting into my car and off we went on an adventure. We rode through every park and subdivision this side of town and then I got this wild idea that I would take them through the airport. This was, of course, before 9-11 and you were free to watch the planes and even talk to the pilot. We watched a pilot start walking toward a ramp to a plane. I asked him if we could look in the plane and he said, "Welcome aboard." I took the two characters into the plane and Ona was just thrilled. They gave him wings and let him see the cockpit. I almost didn't get them off the plane.

Walking back down the corridor, we passed a gift shop and Ona bought a post card to remember his trip. It was at this point that I realized that I didn't have my purse. He had two dollars and spent a dollar-fifty on post cards. We walked back to my car and used what change we could find in the car to pay for parking. I took the rest of his money for parking.

Just outside of the airport, I noticed that I didn't have any gas in my car. I quickly raced to the closest station and started to get gas. What was I thinking? I had no money. I didn't even have a dime to use the phone. My grandfather understood the problem. He was sitting in the front seat and understood that the gas gauge was on empty. Ruth was the only one with money. We tried to ask her to let us use her money to buy gas. She would not give us her purse. A wild boar could not get it away from her. She would scream when one of us would try to get near her. He was trying to tell her that we needed money for gas and that I would give it back to her when we got home. She started cussing at the top of her lungs. Everyone standing around us could hear her dirty little nasty phrase. Somehow I couldn't stop laughing. It looked like I had kidnapped two old people. When the circus was over I went inside and asked the attendant if I could borrow a dime to make a phone call. He gave me the dime and wouldn't you know it, the line was busy. I couldn't get in touch with a soul. My only hope was to try to get the purse. I didn't ask this time, I waited for the right time and distracted her. Ona grabbed her purse and handed me her wallet. Running inside to pay for gas I saw that she had five dollars. This was enough to get us home. My grandfather snuck the purse between the seats and when she started to squeal for it, he said, "It's right there where you left it." I wanted to give him a big high five. Mark one up for Ona!

Mom looked for a nursing home where they could both be placed together. It was just impossible. Most of the homes were full and had a waiting list. The more popular ones were too expensive. They just didn't want to be separated. Ruth's family didn't want to pay that kind of money and her children made it clear that they would not take care of them. Mom was so good to Ruth. She had her hair done each week and bought her new dresses. She loved to go shopping, but not without her Ona. I heard once that her husband was not as kind as my grandfather. Maybe this was the reason there was such a bond. I do know that she was always trying to get him in the bedroom. Off and on all day long she would say, "Let's go lay down, Ona." He would say, "Go on. I'm busy." She would hound him to death until she could get him by herself. One night I had a boyfriend over to watch TV. I was babysitting with them. It was about 9:00 and I thought I had them in bed. Ona opened the door and out he came with a huge whole cut in the front of his pajamas. Well, you can guess what was hanging out all over the place. It wasn't his T-shirt. My friend followed him to the bathroom and pinned his pants together. What a mess. I now knew why she kept trying to get him to take a nap.

Ona continued to go downhill. He was confused and at times didn't know us. He became very incompliant and at times needed to be restrained. Mom did not want to put him in a nursing home. She tried everything to keep the two of them together, but it was just too much for our family. Mom had to call Ruth's daughters to come and get her.

Ruth didn't realize at the time that she was going to be separated forever. I did find a letter recently where she wrote to him telling him she loved him so much and couldn't wait to be together again. Ona couldn't even read the letter much less understand it. I doubt if he would have recognized her. The doctor came to our house and told my mom that it was time to find a nursing home for full-time care. He had lost weight and would drift in and out. When we couldn't get him to eat, the three daughters got together and made a decision to put him in a nursing facility.

I was attending nursing school. I remember stopping by to see him after school and noticed that he would smile, but slept most of the day. Mom was beside herself. She hated the fact that he had to leave her house.

Two weeks later, my aunt Evelyn came to stay the weekend. The doctors said it could be any time and sadly enough, the girls stayed with him one more day and he passed away that night. I remember the last time I spent time with him. He was very agitated and I started singing "Jesus Loves Me" and he calmed down and smiled at me holding my hand. The family was now worried about my aunt Christeen who had just had surgery and was in the hospital.

Once again Mom had to be strong and go into action. She was

in charge of all the funeral arrangements. She called all the extended family and located friends from all of southern Indiana. There was a huge group of people at the funeral home. We all drove back and forth to the little town of Corydon for three days. My grandfather was liked by everyone. His funeral was at the church in town and then he was laid to rest next to my grandmother. Ona had little money. Being the generous person she was, she paid for the funeral. For months she battled insurance companies trying to get all of his medical bills straightened out. Ruth never knew when he died. Her daughters visited the funeral home and that was the last time we ever heard from them until Ruth died a few years later.

Mom was happy to take care of her father. She was always upset that she couldn't take care of him in her home until he died. Ona was a great provider for his wife and children. I know that God was with him till the end. If he knew how bad his health was, he would not have wished for the girls to take on his burden. All three girls honored him always and did what was best for him in his last days.

Deuteronomy 5:16
Honor your father and your mother as the Lord your God has commanded you so that you may live long and that it may go well with you in the land the Lord your God is given you.

Let's All Work Together

There were two days of the year that you knew that you could never plan anything to do on your own. This would be corn day and Labor Day. For some odd reason Mom always thought that she needed to freeze six to eight bushels of corn each summer. She would have Kyle go get the corn and then she would enlist all of the family to gather in her kitchen and put up corn. Some of us would shuck, some silk, Mom would blanch the corn and we would continue to cut the corn off the cob. We always double bagged for freezing. Mom would be very proud of her corn. Everyone who visited our house left with a bag of frozen corn. We had corn for every special occasion.

I hated corn day. Somehow, this was very important to Mom like gathering for Christmas or Thanksgiving. I remember once planning a shopping trip with my friend and didn't realize she had corn coming. She said I planned it, and boy was she mad. I remember that I had to come home early to help so I could keep peace in the family. Even after I was married, I had to come over to do corn. Both of my children grew up with corn day. She could have such a hold on you that you would rather give in than listen to her belittle you for the rest of your life. She would bring it up in conversation and hold it against you at every family gathering reminding you that you were the only one who missed corn day.

Mom also put up beans, tomatoes, peaches, and strawberries.

Cooking together had a special meaning for her growing up. Whenever a family member canned food, they gathered to make it a special time of sharing. We shared every day. Canning did not give us the same satisfaction it gave Mom.

Mom loved to cook and food was so important to her. She never used a receipt and she never gave instructions. She thought you should know how to do things like she did it. She didn't teach us to cook. We just had to watch and learn. She never measured anything. She would add a pinch of this and a cup of that. Then you tasted it to see what was missing.

My job was to make whipping cream and deviled eggs. My sister on the other hand made mashed potatoes and homemade tomato soup. Sarah didn't even try to cook. She hated it all and rightfully so. Most of our time was spent cleaning up after Mom's cooking mess, washing down the kitchen and cleaning the floors. She could not cook without using several pots and pans. Corn day was a sticky mess. It took several hours to clean up after this wonderful occasion.

Another day of the year that we were held hostage by my mom was Labor Day. It was a long weekend and would have been a wonderful time for the family to spend time together doing something fun. Labor Day at our house was "labor day" at the daycare. All the furniture was taken out of the building and the floors were washed and waxed. I can see mom now down on her knees washing the floor in the basement and making me feel guilty that I wanted to make other plans to do something fun. The daycare had to be ready for school and it took all the family to help. You must remember at the age of twenty one, I was the only one at home and my sister also lived in town, so we were the chosen two family members to scrub and clean walls and floors in her last few years of business.

I remember one time I planned to go to the lake with my aunt. My boyfriend was going to take his motorcycle and ride with my aunt and uncle and their friends. We had planned this for a month. It was alright a month ago with mom and the family, but she didn't realize that it was going to be Labor Day weekend. Mom and I argued and I decided to go no matter what she might do to me. I went and when I returned I had such a guilt trip put on me. "How could you go away, knowing your poor mother was on her hands and knees mopping the nursery floors trying to make a living so you can go to college?" It wasn't like I wanted to hurt her, I just wanted a life. Kyle didn't make it any better. He would put things in her head. Anytime she would get upset with me he would try to chime in. His sermon would sound like this, "They should have to work as hard as we did. They don't know what it's like to grow up poor working on the farm stripping tobacco."

The guilt trip made my life miserable. I could never make

decisions on my own. I had to have permission from everyone to do simple things like buying shoes, or going out with friends for lunch. I was always wondering if I was doing the right thing or if I had hurt someone's feelings. **I worried all the time.** My friend and I grew up together in church. We both were in the same situation. I don't know what we would have done if we hadn't had each other to talk to.

Our instinct to survive compels us to avoid pain. I wanted to avoid any pain that I caused at home. I was becoming like my mom. I was basing my self-worth on the approval of my mother and others in my life. It wasn't until years later that I learned that Christ alone is the final authority on my worth and acceptance. He gives me the strength, love, and encouragement I need. In Him I am complete.

Philippians 4:6,7

Do not be anxious about anything, but in everything by prayer and petition, with thanksgiving present your requests to God. And the peace of God, which transcends all understanding, will guard your heart and your minds in Christ Jesus.

Getting Acceptance

At the age of twenty-two I was eager to try new things that would give me the confidence I needed. Some friends and I went to modeling school. I would later model for a local TV morning show. I was so excited. Most mothers would have been excited for their daughter. My mother watched it on TV and said, "You didn't look at the camera enough."

I tried out for Miss Louisville when I was twenty-four. Mom was not supportive. They had mother-daughter teas and luncheons. She never made one of them. She did buy me a very beautiful dress, but never took my picture at the show or after the show. I think Mom was insecure in the way she looked. She always thought she wasn't good enough to be with people who were more educated than her. All I wanted was to have her say I did a good job.

When I would keep asking her opinion on things I accomplished, she would say, "Oh Linda you just want someone to brag on you, don't you?" This would make me feel so bad. Why couldn't she just give me her approval? She was the same way with my sister. When she would sing in church, mom would not react to her. She would say, "So, how was it?" And Mom would reply, "You did just fine" or "I didn't know that song." All we ever wanted was a simple "I am so proud of you."

I truly believe that Kyle made her feel self-conscious. He liked to tell her things that she was doing wrong. He started controlling her every move and this only got worse as she grew older. I longed for the time that we could just sit down as mother and daughter and be friends. This never happened.

When Janice got pregnant with the second child, Mom was excited. It came two months early and weighed just over four pounds. It was a little girl and we were all happy she was going to live. We didn't know if we could love her as much as C.T. but we learned that it wouldn't take long before she became our little sweetheart. Janice took a leave of absence from the school system to stay home with her little girl. She also went to work for mom at the nursery during her time off. Now she was a business partner with Mom. She was happy and willing to help do bookwork and give Mom some rest and time to spend with her new grandbaby. She anticipated that the acceptance from Mom would be abundant.

The Father's Love is full of acceptance. We do not need the approval of our love ones to be accepted by Christ. The Apostle Paul describes God's unconditional acceptance of us.

1 Corinthians 13:4-5
Love is patient, love is kind, it does not envy, it does not boast, it is not proud. It keeps no record of wrong.

Advice in Business

Mom enjoyed having Janice in the business. However, she didn't like having someone give her suggestions on how to run it better. Janice helped her with her books and put together business plans for getting people to pay her on a regular basis. I remember that once she got audited. Mom went hysterical. Her bookkeeping was very shabby and she didn't always show what all she took in on paper. She would come home from work on pay day and hide her money until she could count it. Once she put her deposit for the bank on top of the car ($2,500) while she opened the car door. You guessed it! She drove away with checks and money flying all over the highway. She pulled the car over, and as she was crying she started picking up all of her money and checks. Janice came over and they found all the money. Another time she hid her money in a J.C. Penney's magazine. She forgot that she had hid it there. One day several months later she decided to clean up the magazine rack. She opened up the back door and threw all the books out the door one at a time. Just as she picked up the big heavy magazine and gave it a pitch, all this money and checks started rolling out. She screamed at me to come help her. We were lucky there wasn't a wind. We gathered it all together and she took it to the bank and talked to her friend. I suppose she got it all straightened out. You can now understand why she was so upset with the IRS coming to audit her.

We all prayed that she wouldn't have to go to jail, and Janice and my brother-in-law tried to make sense of all her written records. She didn't like the fact that she had to count all of her cash. Kyle didn't like it either. She made it through the IRS audit and had to pay some back pay; however, Janice reminded her that records had to be kept down to the nickel. Mom found a bookkeeper that was a personal friend and gave her the responsibility of making out payroll. She did a wonderful job and we all stopped worrying until we saw Kyle trying to get "buddy buddy." She was single and he would stop by the business at night when she would do payroll. He would also place himself wherever she was in the building. Sometimes she would do odd jobs for mom at the nursery to earn money and Kyle would just happen to stop by to see if she needed anything. She was doing everything for Mom's benefit and I had no reason to not believe her. She was like family to me, but Kyle could sniff her out wherever she was. She was smart. She wouldn't give him anything from the business. He had the power to write checks and wrote as many as he could get away with.

Janice took care of Mom's personal monthly checks. She would balance her checkbook and had special business checks made so whenever someone wrote a check from the business, it was copied right into the book. Everyone also had to write what was being bought and for what reason. She kept a tight rein on the checkbook so the IRS would have complete records if they ever came back for an audit. Kyle was writing more checks than Mom had suspected. When questioned, he could not recall why they were written. He took out his frustration on Mom. He told her that Janice and her husband wanted to control her money. He suggested that she shouldn't trust her own daughter.

Mom was spending money right and left. She bought boats and a camp on the river. I was glad she was getting rest and enjoying herself. She deserved every penny. I sometimes wondered how he was getting new trucks and expensive tools. He never had any money. If she needed something from the grocery he would ask her for money. He put all of his money in the bank in his account. He continually tried to convince Mom that he was broke. He told her that if something happened to her, he would have nothing to live on. After a while she started to believe him,

Psalm 55:22,23
   Cast your cares on the Lord and He will sustain you; He will never let the righteous fall. But You, O God, will bring down the wicked into the pit of corruption; bloodthirsty and deceitful men will not live out half their day. But as for me, I trust in You.

Success Continues

After I graduated from graduate school, I went to work for my mom teaching kindergarten, hoping something would open in the public school system. I made it the best kindergarten ever. I had lots of new ideas and put all my time into fixing up the new basement. She had once again added onto the building. Mom had a huge classroom dug in the basement under the building that was added six years earlier. This made a huge room for the five-year-olds. On January 24, 1976 a reporter from the local paper came out and took pictures and wrote another article about the daycare. It was a wonderful boost for the business.

Kyle didn't like us girls being in the business. Janice went back to work teaching school. Mom was keeping her baby. I stepped into action working now in the business as the new Kindergarten teacher. Kyle was always calling the employees on the carpet about something. He once complained that I was wasting too much construction paper. He would look in the garbage and report if food was being wasted or girls were coming in late to work. He got on everyone's nerves. The best time Mom and I ever had was when Kyle worked night work. We would go shopping after work and watch what we wanted on TV. When mom and I left work around six at night, we would go to a restaurant and eat supper. It was the freedom that we both enjoyed.

One day I was working in the Kindergarten and mom came to me and told me that she was going to buy the house behind the day care. She said "You know I want you and Janice to have everything I have here, and so I am going to put the property in both of your names. Don't say anything to anyone." It wasn't a big deal to me. I didn't really think much about it. She knew something and she knew what she wanted to do with her money. The new property was going to be used as parking for employees and yard play for the children. Kyle was all excited about the property. He immediately found a renter for the house and started mowing the lawn. Kyle moved his junk in the two sheds on the property and kept his trailer for the boat and mowers behind the house. He enjoyed collecting the rent.

Kyle talked Mom into building a huge garage behind the daycare for his toys. She writes in her diary, *"The big barn was delivered today April 20, 1979. It cost $1,800.00 and $7,243.00 has to be paid to income taxes."* Wow. I know she was trying to figure out how she was going to meet all of her bills. Even though this was a stretch for her financially, she wanted to make him happy. She didn't want him asking any questions about money she had in her account. She would always give him anything he wanted from the business account. He had no idea about paying taxes or meeting payroll.

Mom and Kyle now had a camp, two boats and a huge travel home bought in 1979 for $14,000 to take on vacations. All of this and she still had money on June 7th to buy a new Cadillac. Business was doing well and Kyle was excited.

Mom always gave God a tenth of her earnings and credit for her success.

Leviticus 27:30
   A tithe of everything from the land, whether grain from the soil or fruit from the trees, belongs to the Lord; it is holy to the Lord.

Holding on Tight

I wanted my own life. Mom was so set on me not moving out of the house. In 1976 I got a teaching job and taught for Jefferson County Board of Education in Jefferson County, Kentucky. Mom was upset that I was going to move on, but there was nothing she could do about it. I wanted to start making my own money and I wanted freedom. I saved my money and lived at home. I also worked at the daycare every day after work. I could do any job and substitute for any teacher there. I was not afraid of hard work. I was loved by all the ladies that worked for us. We were all like family. After all, two of them had raised me from birth. Many Fridays I would close the daycare and do the banking so mom and Kyle could go to the lake.

My friend and I wanted to move into an apartment together. We had the money and so we made a down payment and broke the news to our parents. My mom had a fit. She told me I was killing her. How could I be so ungrateful to someone who had given me so much? My friend's mom gave her the same sermon. Our mothers talked on the phone and cried together. We finally gave in and lost our down payment. The guilt was way too much for us. We couldn't live with the two of them giving us so much grief. I hated my life. I was trapped in that house. I worked every day, then worked at the daycare in the afternoons and did lesson plans at night. I was always glad for them to go to the lake on the weekends. It gave me the freedom I needed.

Mom could be so naïve about so many things. I remember when we were little Kyle would try to put his arms around us and it would give me the creeps. He knew I didn't like it so he would hold me tight so I couldn't get away from him. Finally my sister told mom that she hated him touching her and mom got offended and told Kyle not to even try to hug us. Why couldn't she get it?

One Sunday afternoon when Mom and Kyle were out of town,

someone came to the door and I recognized him as the young singer that stayed with mom during a spring revival. I opened the door and he asked if Mom or Kyle was home. When I replied no, he pushed himself inside and said, "You're Linda. I remember you were just coming home from Florida the night we left." I agreed. He said, "You sure are pretty." He told me he wanted to go to church. He asked if it would be alright if he took a shower and got cleaned up. I didn't know what to say. He just took off upstairs and started to take a shower. Thank goodness Mom and Kyle came through the door just as he finished his shower. He was asking for a towel. Kyle took him one.

He asked if he could take me to church. Mom was so excited that a good Christian boy was about to ask me to go to church. I didn't really care, but as long as mom and Kyle were going to church I guess it wouldn't hurt for me to go along. The preacher was glad to see him and asked him to pray.

After church, this boy asked my mom if he could take me to a movie. She was so excited that she said yes right away. He then asked if he could borrow some money. Mom gave him money and we headed toward the gas station. While he was pumping gas I took a look inside his glove box. He had drugs in there. He saw me looking and said he had been sick. He took something and shut the box. Later that night when we came home he tried to sleep in my room. By now I couldn't stand him and I knew what he wanted. I ordered him to his room and slammed the door in his face. He waited ten minutes, and then came begging at my door again. He certainly wasn't talking like a preacher. I am sure he was high. I was so afraid of him. I didn't sleep all night long. Everyone was at work when I left for school the next day. I called Mom from school and told her about him. She said he had gone shopping and wanted more money. He was going to cash a check and bring her back her money. I told her that he was a fraud and she better make sure he was out of the house before I got home. Mom left work and went straight home, and sure enough he had left her high and dry. The next day she got a phone call from an expensive shirt shop telling him that his initialed shirts were ready to be picked up. We never saw him again.

This reminded me of Ona and the street bum. Mom was just like her dad. She always wanted to help the down and out. She gave free housing to many a person. She baked pies and fixed food for the sick. She gave money to the poor and then there was Jim Baker. She always managed to give a seed faith in our names to Oral Roberts and others like Jim Baker who asked for money. God always gave back to her two fold. She prayed for our families to be Christians and go to church. She always worried about her salvation. Mom prayed and when she couldn't pray she would have her friends pray for her.

If you have received Christ as your savior and have lived your life doing his will, you are surly in his hand and cannot be snatched away from him.

1 Peter 5:7
Cast all your anxiety upon Him.

Entertaining

Mom loved having a house full of people. Our youth group usually spent the summer nights at our pool. She could cook up a meal in five minutes with little or nothing. She loved having all of her family at home for Easter and Christmas. We never missed a holiday at her house with a full table and dishes to match. I remember when we got our dish washer. What a wonderful thing to invent. They were so particular with what we could and couldn't put in it. Kyle, of course, had to arrange and rearrange whatever we put inside. You just bit your lip and did everything his way. It was always our job to manage the kitchen and most of the time we were not even allowed to eat at the table with the family. I just knew that if I had a family I, too, would be an adult.

Mom loved Christmas. She would decorate every room in the house. When we were kids we would go to the market down town to buy a real tree and extra evergreen branches to decorate the mantel and the piano. It was such a joy for her to place each little Christmas ornament in its proper place on the end tables and the bay window. She even used real greenery for the stairs, all the way to the top and around the banister. The kitchen had decorated windows and a bright red table cloth. The dining room had gold and silver with bright red candles. Each year she would add to her collection new ornaments, a nativity scene, moving dolls, a Santa that would sing and dance, and lights that sang and blinked. This was a happy time for her.

I remember the last live tree she had in the living room. I was still living at home and mom and I were in the family room watching television. The tree was seven and a half feet tall. It had been decorated with all the old and new Christmas ornaments. Each piece of silver tensile had been hung one piece at a time. Real candy canes were placed on the branches.

Several strings of lights blinked all around the tree. It was beautiful. She was ready to place wrapped packages under the tree. As we were entertaining ourselves in the back room, we heard a loud sound that shook the whole house. It felt like an earthquake. Both of us ran quickly toward the living room. There was the tree. It had fallen across the room landing on the furniture that was in its pathway. Ornaments were broken and the lights were still blinking. I looked at Mom to see if she was going to cry. As she stood there in shock, I started to laugh. I couldn't help but to think of all the work and the weight that was on that tree.

I said, "Where will we put the packages this year?"

Mom had to laugh. The next words out of her mouth were "What will Kyle say?"

I replied, "I don't care. We didn't touch it. We'll just tell him we had an earthquake. I am sure we can convince him to believe us."

Mom called Kyle and he immediately left work to come home and take charge of everything. He had us hold the tree and he put a wire across the room to hold the tree up.

We were ordered to start right away picking up broken glass and loose pine needles. We redecorated the tree, but it just didn't look the same. It was so ugly with that wire strung up. We all complained, but it didn't do any good. He was set on keeping that ugly wire tied to each side of the tree screwed into the wall. I think this was our punishment for putting so many things on the tree. I suggested that we just hang silver tensile on the wire with a few birds. Of course no one agreed. The next year she bought a small white tree and decorated it with all red decorations.

I don't think I could ever estimate how much Mom totally spent on Christmas. She would have several dinners for friends, two different families and employees. She made homemade cookies and pies. She would also make Christmas stockings for each child in the daycare.

The family would make an assembly line and pack bags of candy and oranges to be given out by Santa on the last day of school.

She started Christmas shopping in October and worked right through December 24th. We all made a list for her and she would try her best to give us everything on the list. She would love to surprise us with something that we didn't think we could ever have. She loved to buy for her grandchildren. She loved her babies.

Packages would be piled up all around the tree and out into the middle of the floor. Sometimes it would take us all night to open all of our presents. We would take a break in the middle of the party and eat shrimp and sausage balls. We would finish when someone would knock on the wall and the kids would go out on the porch to see what Santa left.

Until 1977, all of Mom's sisters and their families would join us around the tree at Christmas. We all exchanged gifts. All twenty-five of us. Mom would buy for everyone – nieces and nephews, sisters and brothers-in-laws. It was a wild time but a wonderful fun time. I loved having my aunts and cousins with me at Christmas. We all played tricks on each other and blamed Santa. Mom couldn't be happier. As the family grew, and we all got married we had other families to spend Christmas with so it left just our dysfunctional family. I should say yours and mine. Things were never the same. Kyle's kids and their families sat together and our kids and family sat on the opposite side of the room. Gifts were counted to make sure that everyone was gifted fairly. Mom was a nervous wreck worrying if she got his children and grandchildren enough for Christmas. Whispers and comments were made all over the room. We only saw Ron and his family twice a year so we sometimes gave them gifts that they didn't like. Soon we drew names and made a list. The fun fell out of Christmas.

My husband and children often reminded me that Christmas was about the Christ Child and not about how many gifts we gave on Christmas night. It got so bad that Mom was calling me to see what I had bought people to make sure that my choices were at least one hundred dollars or more per family. She offered to loan me money if I didn't have enough without asking my husband. What a mess!

Luke 2:10-11
The angels said to them, "Do not be afraid. I bring you good news of great Joy that will be for all the people. Today in the town of David a savior has been born to you; He is Christ the Lord."

Empty Nest

In 1980, Sarah got a divorce and moved back home. She found a job and started looking for an apartment. I was steamed. I wanted out! I knew I couldn't move in with Sarah, but I was now twenty-six and wanted to be on my own. I had the money and maybe if I had an apartment in the same building as Sarah, everything would be alright. It was the chance I had to take. I went with her to look at the apartment four blocks down the street from Mom. I was in luck. They had a one bedroom on the bottom floor that was ready to be moved into. I had plenty of money in my account and I made a down payment that very day. I went to see the apartment and was thrilled. I went home and called my sister. For once she was on my side. She understood that I needed my space and said she would help me tell Mom. She came over, and I told Mom I was moving out on Saturday. She was totally upset. I told her it was time. I might not ever get married and I want to get my life together. She knew that I had money and could make the rent. Janice backed me up. Mom didn't say a word to me all night. She was very quiet. I could tell she was sad. Janice went with me to the new apartment and made a list of what I needed to move in.

We cleaned the kitchen and washed down the walls. Mom had nothing to do with any of the cleaning or moving. She just cooked and cried. Kyle was so excited to see me move that he woke me up early on Saturday and started moving my bed out of the room. My uncle came over and helped along with my sister and brother-in-law. That was one of the happiest days of my life. That night I lay on the mattress in my new bedroom and felt so free. I wanted to shout. By the end of the weekend I had my bed up, clothes in the closet and food in the fridge. Mom on the other hand could not even look in my direction when she went to the beauty shop. I got my phone hooked up the next week. Then I called Mom and gave her my number. She never called me, but I am sure she got the information from my sister. Janice went with me to pick out furniture for the living room and the dining room. It was beautiful. I paid cash for all of the furniture. My niece and nephew came and stayed with me and I would take them to K-mart and play school with them. My friend tried to move out but didn't have the same luck I had. She did come over and spend a lot of time with me. I was still lonely, but I was finally free. I had a job, a place of my own, and a car. I still went over and worked at the nursery in the afternoons.

Recently I was reading my Mom's journal and I found the day she wrote about me moving out.

She writes,

January 6, 1980 it's a sad day for me. I cried all day. Linda got an apartment under Sarah. I don't know how I will be able to take it with her moving out.

January 16th Linda is moving out her things. Kyle, Uncle Tom, Janice, and Dewey are all moving her in. I stayed home. I just couldn't go. It hurts to see my baby leave, but if she is happy I'll be happy too.

February 1, Linda got her new furniture and I went over to see it.

It took several weeks before she even came to see my new home. I know in my heart that she loved me. She was so selfish not to let me have a life. It was always all about her. In her next entry of her diary she says that she was so lonesome. Kyle was gone and she was spending all afternoon by herself.

Cooking meals and inviting family over to eat was the sneaky way of getting us all together. I was in no position to say no to her right after I moved out. I felt guilty about leaving her all alone at night and soon she would expect me to come and eat with her every night. She would fix food for me to come by and pick up for supper. She did the same thing to my sister. She wanted to see the grandbabies so she would call and tell her that she had something for them so she would stop by. She loved us girls.

In 1977, I went into the hospital to have a scope of my bladder. The doctor found a malignant tumor. He removed it right away. We were all so thankful that he got it all and I didn't have to have chemo treatments. I did have to have scopes every month and then every year for ten years. Thank God it has never come back. Mom was worried and I saw for the first time the deep down love she had for me. It was the tenderness in her touch and the love and kisses that I will always hold on to. Sadly I didn't get all this affection growing up. My sister was always my rock.

This was the second time the Lord healed my body and gave me life.

Psalm 41:3
The Lord will sustain him on his sickbed and restore him from his bed of illness.

Violet Shows Off Her Business

Mom enjoyed her fishing on weekends, but as I read her diary I see that she loved being back at work on Mondays. I have to admit she was one self-made woman with a strong will. She loved people.

On May 22, 1980, Kyle got the word that his position at work was going to be changed from a foreman to a production worker. The main source of money was coming from the daycare business. Mom was bringing in kids right and left. In 1980, she was averaging 138 full time children. That's not counting after school children, which together totaled around 180 children. In April of 1980, she spent $10,000 on business, home carpet, and contents for repairs for the daycare.

She had a busy year.

Also in 1980, she was elected to serve on the Board of Directors for Community Child Care Centers. This is the committee that measures the quality standards set for all Kentucky daycares. She made several visits back and forth to Lexington to meet with state officials. She served on the board for Private Child Care Centers, attending luncheons, planning service hours for staff and providing information from the state rules and regulations to other owners.

She had several inspectors in and out of her center to see her new additions. This kept her busy making sure that the health records and fire codes were up to date. The spring kept her busy painting, building, and putting in new carpet. The summer was busy with school kids and field trips.

In August 1980, she paid $44,200 to have her driveways paved at the daycare. Classrooms were put together with supplies and new equipment. The playground had new rock delivered and the staff was called in to prepare for the new school year. Each year she wrote a note to the parents welcoming them to the center and giving them a handbook for the year.

With all of this work going on at the day care, she still found time, in August of the same year, to have Kyle's family over for a big birthday party for Kyle's mother. The family never brought food. She always made sure that she cooked everything. The group numbered over twenty-five. In September she got the school year up and running. In November, she left for Florida to go fishing and to visit Disney World. When she returned she had an open house for the daycare parents. In December she had a Christmas dinner for her employees, a huge Christmas dinner for Kyle's family and then all of the immediate family came over for Christmas dinner on Christmas Eve.

I find it humorous that Mom writes in her journal,

I had a wonderful Christmas, but I didn't go to church today. My eyes are so swollen and I look terrible. I guess I'll fix dinner for the kids and have them come over after church.

Mom just couldn't go on running like this year after year. The doctor told her back in January, 1980 that she had high cholesterol. He gave her some medicine and told her to watch what she was eating. She never got any exercise. She left the day care on Fridays and spent the weekends at the lake fishing.

Her family meant everything to her. Reading her daily journals helped me understand that her love for her sisters and her children was the only thing that mattered in her life. She loved Kyle, but not like a lover. He didn't know how to love her back.

She wanted to be in control of her family. Kyle wanted to be in control of her. She knew he needed her to live. He knew that without her income he could not have the lifestyle he was used to. Mom had put his son through college and graduate school, sending money when needed. She loved Sarah and Sarah loved her. Mom would give Sarah anything she needed. It was kind of sad to see that she could not express her love for her family. She put a lot of importance on things. She knew that she had you in her grips because you needed her for things. She didn't understand that we needed her love more.

I wanted to shout, "Love me for who I am!" That is all I ever wanted from her. When I confronted her on something she did wrong, it would offend her. She would say, "How can you tell me that after all I do for you?" You could not argue with her. She always had the last word.

Thank You, Lord Jesus for the comfort and love you give me when others seem far away.

Judges 20:22
But the men of Israel encouraged one another and again took up their positions.

The Heart Attack Continues

It was October, 1981. Mom had been to the doctor for a checkup and as usual he told her to lose weight and get her cholesterol under control. She had just finished a busy two months getting her school year under control. New children were beginning to settle into their new surroundings. She was training new teachers, dealing with new parents. The stress was taking over her life even though she didn't realize it. We all knew that she was worn out and over worked. Kyle never gave her a break. He would always say we need to do this, that, and the other, always reminding her that she needed to be working. She became a very good worrier along with Kyle.

The daycare was killing her. A new two year old child had been bitten by another new two year old. When the father of the child picked up the baby, he was very upset with the teeth marks on his child. He said it better never happen again and Mom tried to explain that they didn't know that the new child was a biter. She promised that the children would be separated.

A few days later when the children were eating snacks, a substitute teacher placed the two children next to each other and sure enough, the two-year old biter, bit the other two year old up and down the arm leaving several bite marks. When the teacher took the child to the office to Mom, she got very upset. She lay on the floor and cried like a baby. She started having chest pains and couldn't breathe. Janice just happened to come in the door to pick up her kids and saw Mom lying on the floor crying. While Mom had regained her composure, Janice called the parent and confessed the truth about what had happened. She told her that it was a mistake and that the other parent was going to be told to remove the two year old from the daycare. After talking to the parent and explaining what happened, the mother came over and seemed to understand. As it turned out, this parent became fond of the daycare and cried when her child had to leave the center six years later to go to first grade.

Mom was now having chest pains off and on every day. This paved the way for the two heart attacks she suffered on that October day in 1981.

Things didn't look good. She was left unconscious as we took turns going back to see her. I never felt so alone in my life, with no one to turn to except the arms of my sister and aunt. I wanted to be loved and consoled. My friends visited me a few days later, and took me home and spent the night with me. It was that night that I received my first phone call from my future husband. The phone rang as my girl friends sat on the couch trying to console me.

I answered the phone. "Hello?" My voice was so weak from crying that I could hardly make a sound.

"Hello." said the voice on the other end. "Is Linda there?"

I replied in a soft voice, "Yes. This is Linda."

"My name is Richard. I am a friend of Victoria and she gave me your phone number."

"Oh! Yes," I said.

"Is this a good time to call?" He replied.

I tried to talk, but my voice got weaker. "I am sorry but my mom just had two heart attacks this week and I have cried so much that I don't have a voice."

"I am so sorry," he replied, "Maybe I should call back again sometime."

"Yes, that would be great!" I knew that my friend was going to fix me up with an old classmate, but now was not the time to meet someone new. I took a chance that he may never call back, but I had faith that God would somehow answer my prayer that I would meet a Christian guy my age.

When Mom was able to carry on a real conversation I told her about my phone call from Richard. For once in her life, she seemed interested in what I had to say. Mom and my friend were concerned about my lonely life. They had talked several times on the phone about Richard. Mom was now ready for me to meet someone nice. She knew more about him than I did. We talked about where he lived and how we went to school together. I was totally surprised that she was so involved in the conversation. Sometimes I feel that this is what kept her alive. She now had a mission to control my dating life and to get me married.

Mom came home from the hospital and had to change her whole lifestyle. My sister and I had to change our lifestyles as well. We went to the daycare and regrouped the staff. We had a meeting telling them that we were going to take a leave of absence from the school system and run the center. Most of the staff was excited. We grouped kids according to age and ability. We made new rules about keeping daily logs on each child. We wrote notes to parents telling them that we were the new directors and that we expected that there would be little or no changes. Everything we did was to improve the center and the way it was run. We were able to get money that was owed and set up new programs to get money from the state. This was a lot of paper work for Janice, but we did get the money that was owed to us. We were so proud that we were able to stop our jobs and take care of Mom and her business. I remember the conversation Janice and I had in the hospital.

"Linda, it looks like mom won't be able to go back to work for a long while. You know that the staff must be paid and the business must go on as usual. We would have to hire a director or leave our jobs to be the director until mom gets better."

"What if she doesn't get better?" I replied.

"Well, we can just take a leave and see what is going to happen. You know that there are several people that Kyle would like see take over the business. He wants to get in control of Mom and the business. If this happens we will lose all the staff that has been true to Mom all these years."

We knew Mom was so naïve to suspect him of doing anything that was not in her best interest.

Matthew 24:4,5

Jesus answered, "Watch out that no one deceives you. For many will come in My name, claiming, 'I am the Christ,' and will deceive many."

Save the Business

Mom was having therapy for her heart attack twice a week. This kept Kyle busy during the day and he worked night work so we had a chance to make an office for working on paperwork and rearrange staff for morning and afternoons to fit the growing needs of the students. We kept everything in order, receipts made for all money taken in and checks written out.

Christmas came and went. We had a party for the staff, and then we made the decision that we would leave our jobs and stay at the business full-time. I became responsible for the kindergarten building which housed fifty children. Janice took the position as director of the main building.

We had thirty-two girls working full and part time. The state had now made it a law in 1981 that all directors must have a degree in education or be in business for more than twenty years. The private kindergarten must have a degreed teacher to meet the requirements of the public school system. My degree was in Elementary Education and early childhood education with a special degree in kindergarten. We were more than qualified to meet the needs of the center.

The word spread quickly that we were one of the top private daycares in Louisville. Teachers, doctors and other professionals wanted to get their children in our center. We were so proud of the new educational curriculum we revised for each age group. We listed ages and stages of development on each classroom wall. We bought new age appropriate toys that went along with the curriculum. We required each teacher to have lesson plans and keep records of progress for each child. We wrote a newsletter once a month to the parents telling them about the events going on in the classroom. We held open houses. We took field trips. It was a lot of hard work but we were so proud of our effort to make the center the best in Jefferson County. We now had five busses stopping in front of the business returning school children to our center after school.

Things were great at the center. Mom's health began to improve so Kyle had more time to spend in our building. He would come early in the mornings and chat with the girls and hang out listening to all the gossip. He would report who came in late and who was living with men not married. He would watch each girl where they parked. In fact he assigned parking spaces. Any bit of news that came in the back door he would take home to Mom. He would get her so upset. She would call us on the phone and say, "Did you know so and so was dating a black guy? Did you know so and so was coming in with her child and putting it on the bus in the mornings? You girls should get there early so you can see what is going on around there." He even reported what time we got to work. He told the staff that they should call him if they had problems with the buildings structures or plumbing. Mom wanted the front desk receptionist to know that Kyle was still in control of the buildings and she was in control of us.

It was so hard to remain quiet and be excited about the job. We wanted so much for her to see what a good job we were doing. Instead of praise we were told that it was our fault that she left the daycare. She didn't like any of the new changes we made in the structure of the business. She didn't want to see that the center was growing faster each month. She loved the money that she received for doing nothing. She could not relate the increase in money to the new changes in running the business. Kyle was always reporting negative things and situations to Mom. He would tell her that children were left alone without teachers, and food was being wasted. Anything he said she would believe and reprimand us by noon of the same day. She would always send him over to get bread for the center in the mornings. She would have the office call her house and tell Kyle what they needed before we arrived in the morning. She would send him to fix the water fountain and cots, anything that would keep him in sight of what was going on in the center. Mom felt that it was important that Kyle feel needed in the center.

It was so frustrating to us girls. We were working for three hundred dollars a week and took a big cut in pay from the school system to keep her business going. We doubled her income and kept all the paper work in place. She didn't have to do a thing but collect the money each week. Later as she started to decline in health, we sent her a staff member to take care of her and paid her from the earnings of the daycare. Kyle got a gas allowance weekly. We did everything she wanted us to do. She knew we were doing an excellent job, but she just couldn't tell us to our face.

It was a daily routine that we went to work and took off at naptime to have lunch at her house across the street. This was the time of truth or dare. She would tell us about what she heard and dared us to say that Kyle was not telling the truth. We would try to make it just a time to be with her, a time to talk about ourselves and how she was feeling. We always had Kyle there listening to everything we were saying to her. It got so bad that we would try to wait until he went to the drug store or grocery to go and talk girl talk to her. Sometimes he would fake leaving and go downstairs to listen to what we were saying. He wanted to see if we were talking about him. We would take her out to lunch and Kyle would get mad. Soon she was inviting him to join us. He did not like for us to be alone with our own mother. We knew something was up but couldn't put our finger on it. Later we would find out that he would take the checks for bread and write them for more than it cost and keep the change for himself. We also found out that he had an IRA that he couldn't account for. So what! It wasn't any of our business. But he would lie about having money and make Mom feel sorry that he was so broke.

Lying to each other disrupts unity by creating conflicts and destroying trust. It tears down relationships and leads to open warfare.

Ephesians 4:25
Therefore each of you must put off falsehood and speak truthfully to his neighbor, for we are all members of one body.

A Wedding for Linda

I started going out with Richard in December of 1981. We were married the next year in October of 1982. Mom was excited about my marrying Richard. She got to know his mother and they became good friends. Mom and I would go out to eat with Richard and his parents on Friday nights. She seemed like her old self again. She had some new friends. We would talk about the wedding and make plans. Mom took me out to buy my wedding dress. We went to a bridal shop and found the dress right away. Then we looked for her a dress. She picked out a pale pink dress but couldn't decide if she really wanted to buy it. As soon as she put the dress back on the rack, another lady picked up the dress and mom pitched a fit. She said, "Oh, excuse me miss, but you have my dress." I thought they were going to fight for a minute. Mom tried to explain that she had just set it down to pick up another dress. I was at the side laughing and waiting to see who would win. Mom was talking her way out of the whole situation and, of course, she won! I said, "Well I guess we know what dress you will be wearing." Mom looked around and couldn't find anything she liked better. We laughed about the dress on many occasions. Mom told me that she looked so good in the dress that she wanted to be buried in it. The day she died we found the dress and she got her wish.

I didn't want Kyle to walk me down the aisle. I tried to tell Mom my wishes, but she wouldn't listen. She said people would talk. "Besides, he has been there in your daddy's place all these years." I wanted to say, "No, he never treated me as a daughter. He was jealous of me and has taken you away from me. He has stood in the way of my freedom of speech and my ability to take control of my own life. He had a negative attitude toward any opinion I would voice. He has turned you into a negative controlling person who is obsessed with money and people taking advantage of you." He didn't like Mom having friends. Her only close friends were at the beauty shop. He didn't like going out with my in-laws. He was jealous of my father-in-law.

The wedding was set and took place as planned. There were over 500 people in attendance. I just knew being married would change everything. I now had the love of my life and felt that I would no longer be controlled by Mom and Kyle.

When we arrived home after the honeymoon Mom had a big surprise planned for us at her house. We opened gifts, but I knew she was not happy about something. Later she said she thought that I should have called her on my honeymoon. I did call her once, but didn't realize that I needed to call every day. I went back to work and found out that nothing had changed. She treated me like a child. She said I didn't know how to cook well enough for Richard. She would check on me every night to see what we had for supper. I remember cooking four and five dishes every night. Richard finally told me that I didn't have to cook so much every night. He said he loved leftovers and that we should eat what we had. I tried very hard to make him happy. I was also trying to make Mom happy. I would spend lots of time on the phone at night with Mom or Janice talking about the business. Sometimes Mom would call me two or three times a night after I got home from work. I was still trapped. If I failed to tell her we were going somewhere at night or over the weekend, she would get upset. When we would finally talk, her conversation would start like this, "Well, did you forget that you had a mother over here?" We would have a date night on Friday night and stop by her house before we went home. I don't know how my husband put up with all the dysfunction in our family.

Richard was a Christian and that was in my favor. I knew he must truly love me if he could overlook the problems in the family.

Ephesians 4:2-3
Be completely humble and gentle; be patient, bearing with one another in love. Make every effort to keep the unity of the Spirit through the bond of peace.

Give Us Trust

Whenever we would have monthly business meetings with the other day care owners, we would take Mom with us so she could be with her friends. Mom liked to bring up a discussion about rules and regulations set by the State.

She knew how things changed and what was expected of her in the past. She would get on her soap box about the State and get a huge discussion going among the long time owners. Mom would put us down in front of her friends by saying, "Janice and Linda do everything the inspectors tell them to do. They don't question the ladies like I did. They certainly do things a lot different." We would look at each other and wonder why! After all we had done to build up her business. Why would she make fun of us in front of her friends? She would also say things like, "I guess you have to have a fancy education now to do all the things we did years ago without one." It was true. Education had changed and some of the older owners of private daycares did not want to attend continued educational classes four times a year. Most of these centers were not up to date with the rules and wanted to protest against the state. Janice and I worked late into the evening to count money and hash out the problems of the day. We wanted to do this after work and not at her house at noon. If our cars were at the office building later after we closed, she would call us and ask what was going on. She could not stand for us to make any decisions without her knowledge.

Years ago, I was asked to teach childcare workers when I received my master's degree in early childhood. Janice and I continued to teach adult education classes that other centers protested against. In meetings Mom would take their point of view. She felt that these classes were not important to centers that had been in business for over twenty years. Mom could not see that she had two daughters who had master's degrees in education and were well aware of what the other directors lacked in their centers. Instead she would get mad because we paid for educational courses for the staff and sound off because we didn't share in her protest against the state. Eventually we were asked to give three hour introductory courses for all new people working in a preschool or private center. We were paid by the state and spent hours putting together information and videos teaching classes of 60 or more all over Louisville. This also benefited our center because we held many classes at our place and didn't have to pay for the new staff we employed. Having a large staff, could be expensive for the business, so doing educational classes helped out our budget. Still we were working for $300 dollars a week and maybe a bonus.

We wanted Mom to be a part of what we were doing. We asked her almost on a daily basis to come over and work in the office. We felt that this would help her to get out of the house and feel like she was needed. It would also give her back some of her self-confidence that Kyle took away when she was sick. He kept telling her that she couldn't do things. He wanted her to feel like she needed him for everything. He wouldn't let her drive, or walk outside by herself. She became very insecure. She wouldn't walk on her treadmill without someone there. She was constantly taking her pulse and blood pressure. When she left the house she had panic attacks. Many nights she would call us over to her house to sit with her because she thought she was going to have another heart attack.

Mom could not trust that God was in control of her life. She would pray for God to heal her, but she didn't fully give up the worry that consumed her whole life.

Psalm 9:9
The Lord is a refuge for the oppressed, a stronghold in times of trouble.

Mind Games

All the moxie she had all of her life was being sucked out of her by this negative man who was playing with her mind and money. He had a plan to turn her against us. He made up stories that were not true and reported them to her. He made her believe that we were taking the coke machine money. He reported that we were paying for weekly sanitation machines in bathrooms and monthly pest control that was not necessary. Little did he know that we had termites in the office and the sanitation machines were given to us on a trial basis to see if it would cut down on germs and smells in the center's bathrooms. We were always trying to explain ourselves. There were so many times we wanted to quit and give her back the control of the business. We knew that she couldn't take any of the pressure that the huge business demanded. It was all we could do to keep everyone happy and organized.

She now owned a small school. We offered gym and swim programs at the YMCA, speech theory, computer tots, and physical activity with the gymnastic bus. We had to keep up with the children who were enrolled in each special program. There was no way she could keep up with all the new changes. Yet she continued to tell everyone that leaving the business was the worst thing she ever did. She said she should have never given us control of her business. I know she didn't mean anything she was saying. She would use this when Kyle would get her so worked up about something we did or didn't do. Believe me she was still in full control of the business.

In 1985, I had a baby boy. He was beautiful and Mom adored him. He was sick a lot and so Mom wanted to keep him at her house so he wouldn't be exposed to all the germs brought in by other children. This was a good change for her. It kept her focused on something besides herself. We shared him with her as much as possible. She would fix supper for us all after work. During supper she would share all the cute things he did all day. It was like she now had another reason to go on living. We still visited her at lunch and let her know everything that was going on in the daycare. She started to say thank you for the small things she noticed that we were doing to improve the property and the business. Once again she saw us as family and not enemies. Things would go along well for maybe a month and then she would again focus on what was missing in her life. She needed the control of the business. We encouraged her to go fishing on the weekends and go on trips with her sister. She loved to go fishing with Kyle and her sister and her husband. They would take long trips to Canada and Florida. These were the happiest times of her life. She enjoyed a weekend of fishing and being with her sister Christeen. What freedom we felt with her gone. We were still working very hard, but we didn't have to deal with the daily questions.

In 1988, I had another son. I worked right up to the time he was born. Both of my children were born in June, so I didn't have to take off during the school year. Things seem to be going along well. We still had to deal with Kyle but we tried to get around him and keep peace in the family. He was now going on day work some and it helped us to work without friction. Mom was getting weaker and weaker. She was hospitalized many times for congestive heart failure. She liked for us girls to go to the doctor with her.

She liked for us to be with her whenever we could. She was clinging to us and her grandchildren. We always went to the doctor with her when Kyle was gone or unable to go. She knew we would get the diagnosis right and be able to explain it to her after we left the doctor's office. Of course, we had to list all her medications for her and Kyle. He liked to have control over her medicines and would sometimes tell us that she was taking too much. We couldn't always tell if he was telling us the truth. Sometimes she would sleep all day and be drowsy when she wasn't sleeping. We wondered if he gave her something to sleep or if she was over medicating her own self.

Psalms 10:2,4

In the arrogance the wicked man hunts down the weak, which are caught in the schemes he devises. In his pride the wicked does not seek Him. In all his thoughts there is no room for God.

Family Ties

She was beginning to understand that there was no way she could continue to work in such bad health. She was now approaching her eighties and reality was setting in. She wanted her family to go to the lake with her and spend the weekend. My boys loved to ride in their boat and try to fish. Mom sure got a kick out of them. She would make up stories about the fish they caught. They would ride in the golf cart down to the water and enjoyed walking up to the small store to get ice cream.

Mom and Kyle took the whole family on vacation to Disney World, Janice's family, Sarah's family and my family. Mom was in a wheelchair, but this did not stop her from having a wonderful time with all her children and grandchildren. We took the big RV and stayed in a hotel that was right on the edge of the park. The grandkids enjoyed riding in her lap in the wheelchair and we also did not have to wait in long lines for rides. I believe that Mom was beginning to realize that her life was growing shorter. She now wanted to spend time with her grandchildren. I also believe she was onto Kyle, but knew that she still needed him to take care of her. She wanted the families to get along and she wanted the kids to love both she and Kyle as grandparents. Little did she know that the grandchildren had already taken a dislike to Kyle. He was always yelling at them and bossing them around. We tried to make sure that they respected him and did what he asked.

I tried so hard to remember the vacations away from home and the times Mom would turn loose and just be herself. Mom could have a lot of fun if she was given permission.

One time she told me there were two things she hated to do. "What's that Mom?" I asked. "I hate to floss my teeth and change the toilet paper roll in the bathroom."

"Add dishes to that hate list, Mom," I replied. "You never liked to do the dishes."

"Oh, I suppose I could if I had to." Mom hated housework. She enjoyed reading, politics, the nightly news and being outdoors on a sunny day, especially if it was in a boat, fishing. We tried to explain to her that it was now her time to do all the things she had ever wanted to do. "You have the money and the time. Go for it, Mom. Let us run the business. You sit back and enjoy the money." We talked to an accountant friend of my sister's and she showed us how we could get money for rent. We showed Mom new ways to get more for her money. She knew that we were trying to do what was best for her and it seemed to finally sink in.

God is faithful and just. When we put our trust in Him, He quiets our heart. We can trust Him in times of trouble.

Psalm 6:2
Be merciful to me, Lord, for I am faint; O Lord, heal me, for my bones are in agony.

Unfaithful

In 1998, we hired a new girl for the two-year-old program. She was very attractive and sweet. Her husband had been in the daycare when he was younger. She had been there about a week when her husband came into the office and wanted to talk to Janice. "Sure," she said, "Come on in the office and sit down. What can I do to help you?"

"Well, this is a little awkward, but my wife is not going to be able to work here anymore."

"Why?" she asked.

"Well, yesterday when she was putting clothes in the washer downstairs, Kyle pushed her back against the washer and asked her to give him a kiss. She is scared, and I don't want her to be here with him."

Janice was so surprised and shocked. "I'll take care of that. You do what you need to do. I totally understand and I'll make sure it never happens again in this business. He is not employed here and should not be in the building when we are open for business. This is the first time I have ever had a complaint."

"I am not lying," said the man, "she's pretty upset!"

"I understand!" said Janice. "I am sorry. Like I said, do what you have to do. If you want to file charges against him, I'll understand."

Janice was sure upset. She called me to the office and we had a long talk about the problem. This was the first time anyone had said anything about him trying to touch them. What were we going to do?

Kyle needed to be out of the business, but Mom would not let us keep him away from the business. She knew he would get mad and be upset with her.

She told us, "Kyle was always there in the business. I'm still in control and the business is still in my name, so Kyle will not be banned from the building. I don't want him to think I am taking him away from the daycare."

She made sure he was involved in cutting the grass, painting and maintaining the building. If our husbands came over to fix something she would get very upset.

The problem with Kyle and the staff was a big concern. We learned that he was coming over to the center in the morning and having coffee when the staff arrived before we opened. He would make every excuse to be there when we had a full staff. He would go to the storage basement, hang out in his big barn or work out in the yard to watch everything that went on around there. We would never know when or where he was going to pop up.

Fighting it with all our might, we made the decision to talk to Mom. We found a time when he was away at the lake and we went over to tell her about the new employee. Of course she did not believe us. We asked her if there was any way we could keep him from coming to the center during working hours.

She had a fit! "No way! He has always been there and he has always been a part of the business. I couldn't do him that way. That is part of his life."

"Mom, we don't want to keep him away from the center, we just want him to stay away from the staff. They feel uncomfortable around him," I replied.

Mom said, "That girl is lying and you are just taking it out on Kyle. I have never heard one complaint from any of the old girls who were there when I was there."

Little did she know that her own brother-in-law would not let her own sister ride with Kyle to the store by herself. The office lady would not let her husband know that he was there in the office during the day. Mom would not listen to us. The only reason that the young lady didn't press charges was out of respect that her husband had for Mom. We explained that there was a witness that saw her run out of the room and he came out after her. She would have had a good case. We explained all of this to Mom, but she would not listen. Instead, she talked to Kyle and told him what we said and, of course, he denied the allegations of the young girl. He told her that we wanted him out of the picture so we could take over her money.

What a mess we were in. Now he hated us even more.

He would get us back… and he did.

Kyle was still having his coffee and conversation with the morning girls. He loved to spread gossip, especially if it was of interest to Mom. He stayed out of our way and would hardly speak to us for about a month. Mom would send him to pick up our kids at school or do something for us as if we were trying to say we were sorry and we wanted him back into the building. It wasn't long before he was right back to his old ways. Mom would have us over for lunch and try to smooth things over. We had to drop the whole issue and continue to work as if nothing had ever happened.

One day, Mom tried to wash clothes in the basement. She got down on her bottom and scooted down the stairs. She started looking around, and boy did she have a surprise. He had all kinds of things going on down there. She hadn't been in the basement for years. He had collected a lot of stuff that he was selling on the side. The basement was a mess. She started looking through all the new junk and found some old shoes. She picked up the shoes, and in the toe of the shoes there was money. Lots of money! He had been hiding money where he knew she would never find it. Mom was surely on to him at this point. She shared this information with her sister. She later shared it with us girls. Mom knew he was up to something, but she had no way of following him and catching him like she did Daddy. She was tired and decided that whatever she did he would leave her and she would not have anyone to take care of her. We knew what kind of a character he was, but what were we going to do? He held all the cards now. She had bought him a new boat, a truck, a new house on the lake, and he bought anything he wanted with her money. He would talk her into whatever he said they needed.

Mom started getting her financial matters in order. She would say to us girls, "I want you two to have the daycare if something ever happens to me." We told her that as long as everything was in her name he had every right to all she had. She just couldn't believe us. We made an appointment with a CPA and he explained that she needed a will. This would help her to tell the girls just what she wanted them to have at her death. He also said that Kyle needed a will. So Mom went to Kyle and told him that they needed to make out wills. He was not a happy camper. He began to question her. He blamed everything on us girls. We assured him that we did not want to take anything that Mom did not want us to have. Mom saw right then that he had hate for us. She still wanted control. To make things fair, it was decided that all our spouses sign an agreement. The agreement said that if something happened to Mom, Janice or me, equal parts of the business would go to the surviving family members. None of the spouses would be included in the partnership of the money. This way we would inherit the business like Mom wanted. Our husbands felt that it was fair. Kyle on the other hand was not very happy. He signed the papers and then he made out his will. All of his assets were to go to his kids not Mom.

He had a big bank account and they had an account together. He had two IRAs that she took out for him. He didn't even know how to write out a check when she married him. She always paid for everything. She paid all the bills. She began to watch her money very carefully. We set it up that she got a paycheck every Friday. Sometimes she would have us cash the check and hide it from him. What a way to live. She soon gave us a little raise and took money out of the account to buy diamond rings for herself. She had new wedding rings, solitary rings and whenever she could she would buy us diamond bracelets for Christmas and our birthday. She knew she was going to have a fight on her hands with him when it came to money. He had his eyes on everything in her purse. He knew that he now had to come to us to get money from the business. He didn't have the privilege of getting money anytime he wanted right out of the cash register.

The daycare was doing well in the 1990s and the family was continuing to save face in front of friends. You would never know that a storm was always brewing inside the house. Year after year we continued to work the business and it continued to grow. Mom kept a diary everyday telling us about the weather, the amount of fish she caught at the lake and who she had spent time with. She loved to write about her family visiting. It got harder and harder to visit with her. When you left her house you were always depressed. She would unload her problems on us. Mostly she was concerned with her health. Kyle kept telling her that she needed to rest.

She writes in 1995,

What a day I am having. Up awhile then I sleep awhile. Don't know what is wrong. Kyle has gone to the lake and I am here by myself. I just have a feeling I can't last long. My heart seems good. I just can hardly write I'm so shaky.

He wanted to keep her questioning her health. I wonder sometimes if he didn't give her something to sleep while he was away.

Weeks later, she writes,

I had a wonderful Thanksgiving. Everyone was here and we had to put up an extra table. We went to the playhouse to see my grandson perform in the play, <u>Home for Christmas</u>. I had a wonderful time. There were 20 family members here for Christmas dinner. We all had a wonderful time. I gave Kyle a beautiful diamond ring he wanted.

Mom seemed like a different person.

She was now getting $2,000 a month for rent plus her weekly paycheck of over $900. This was on top of her Social Security. Kyle retired from his job. This meant that he would be home all day long. Mom started to get more and more depressed. She talks about her health nonstop. The only thing she looks forward to is her grandchildren visiting.

One morning an employee came into the office and said she needed to talk to Janice. She told her that she walked into the baby room and found Kyle and another staff member kissing in the bathroom. She said he was there to change the light bulb. The employee was in her late sixties and so she was quite concerned at what she saw. She was crying and upset for Mom.

"What should we do?" she replied.

Janice kept her in the office and had her go over everything again. "Maybe you didn't see what you thought you saw," she said.

"Oh no, it is true, they were upset with me for catching them."

As the news spread throughout the daycare other ladies started to confess. One said that he called her from his night job and asked her to meet him at 11:30 when he got off work. One lady said that he tried to hold her down on the table and kiss her while she was feeding the kids. She said she almost slapped him with the carton of milk. Now what?

Janice called me into the office and we had a long talk. We needed him out of the business and soon. How do we tell Mom?

She will never believe us. He was still chasing the employees and making fools out of us. We caught him in many lies.

Mom was having a hard time walking and breathing. She got tired easily. We knew if we told her anything about Kyle that she would certainly try to reject the fact that he was unfaithful to her. He had her so snowed that he could go anywhere and do anything he wanted. He would get up early and go to breakfast or wherever in the morning before she could even get out of bed. She had to wait for the caregiver to come and help her get dressed. He also controlled her medicine and had coffee ready for her before he left for his morning outing.

I will have to say that she was controlling as she became more dependent on someone doing things for her. She would order us all around. "Get me my shoes, my glasses, paper." He made her so dependent on everyone. He liked the fact that she was weak and needed him. Sometimes I would feel sorry for him because he was there taking orders from her, but then I had to remember that he could disappear whenever he wanted and would always appear with an alibi that made perfect sense to everyone.

Mom slept every afternoon after lunch. I would see him slip off down the highway in his little red truck. Who knows where he was going? We caught him in several lies. He would fish around and hated it whenever anyone would catch him lying. He would throw a fit and slam the back door and peal out of the drive. The hate for us girls was so real that you could feel the tension in the air. Mom was still trying to save face for us. She would call us on the phone and say, "Ask Kyle to pick up the kids from school. Ask Kyle to help Richard." We did anything we could to keep peace. Our husbands were always good to him. They made sure that they shopped for him at Fathers Day and Christmas. They asked for advice for projects and were always respectful to him no matter what kind of garbage he would pretend to know about something. They knew how hard it was on us. They saw what was happening. They knew the score. The negative feelings would flow from the house as we would try to walk in and cheerfully try to joke about the events of the day.

The problem with the employees had to be addressed. But how? How do you tell your mother that the second man she trusted was a bum and unfaithful to her? We waited for several days. We talked about it for hours. How were we going to get him away from the daycare? Why was he kissing this divorced woman? He was truly trying to get what he wanted from her. Why did he call others from work? He was a fake. He knew what he was doing. This was not a mistake. He really wanted to harass the girls and see who might be interested in him. Time and time again we would run this through our brain and think of nothing else but what we should do about Kyle. What if she didn't believe us? It was hard to act normal around her while keeping this deep, dark secret.

We took her long time employee and care giver out for a ride. We questioned her about his activity. She said she had never noticed anything. She said she had heard stories, but didn't believe he would do anything like that to Violet. It upset her so much that we thought that maybe she knew something, but didn't want to get involved. After all, she had worked for Mom for over thirty years. We did however know that she did not like to be at the house if he was going to be there alone with her. She said she didn't like the thought of cleaning the house with him around. She would not give any reason for her actions. She said she just didn't like men being around.

We questioned the employee once again and she was certain about what she saw. She pleaded for us not to hurt Miss Violet. As the weeks and days passed, he would come and go as he wished in and out of the center. Watching him drove us crazy. One of our church members worked in the three-year-old room and had heard the rumor. She called us to her side and told us that he had flirted with several employees. She said that something really needed to be done about him. She confirmed the story that another lady told us about the lunch table. Things were beginning to line up.

I talked to my husband about the problem and he thought that we should forget it. My brother-in-law was of the same opinion. We listened to them, but what do they know? They are both men. Mom was now in her eighties and another heart attack is not what she needs. We were both afraid to face him. Who knew what he would do to us! We didn't trust him. So when the time was right, and he was out of the house, we approached Mom with the information. We asked her not to tell Kyle just yet. She sat and looked at us as if we were crazy. She stared into space for a long time. She asked questions.

Then she said, "I want her to tell me what she saw. I think she is lying."

She didn't believe us. We tried to tell her that we just wanted to keep him away from the business and we didn't want trouble in the family.

She would have it her way.

"NO! I want to hear it for myself."

So we took her to the nursery and we talked to the little old lady who was scared to death. She was so frightened that she almost passed out. Mom confronted her in a way that would have put the FBI to shame. She almost had her to admit that she didn't see what she thought she saw. After about five minutes or so of Mom's intimidating questions, the employee begins to cry.

"I don't want to lose my job, Miss Violet. Maybe he was just changing the light bulb." We told her to tell the truth.

She said." Yes I did see him, but I don't want to cause any trouble."

Mom left the room and we consoled her and told the employee she did the right thing by telling the truth.

Mom could never keep a secret. She confronted Kyle as soon as he came home. In her heart of hearts I know she knew what was coming down. She just didn't want to admit it. She listened to him blame us for the rumor. They sat up all night long with him telling her that we wanted him and her out of the business so we could get her money. He told her that we spent all of her money on the daycare without her knowing it. He said we went shopping for expensive things that the business didn't need. We had too many girls working for us and that we were taking money on a daily basis for ourselves. He filled her up with lies and said he saw lots of things going on around there that he could tell about, but he didn't want to upset her. He even told her that our husbands were putting things in our heads and they were trying to take over.

Mom called us in a rage the next morning. She said we were traitors and that we wanted to kill her. Why did we make up such a story? Kyle loved her and she knew for a fact that he would do anything for her. Didn't we understand that she needed him? Would either one of you come over here and clean me up when I get sick. I can't see you leaving your families to take care of me. I can't stay by myself. You have your family and I am not going to believe lies so you can get rid of Kyle. Your husbands are behind this aren't they?

She had gone crazy. "What in the world are you talking about?" I replied, "You have got to be kidding me. My husband has his own business and his own money. We don't need your money. Why in the world did you discuss this with Kyle?"

"He loves me and he told me that he would never do anything like that to hurt me. You two girls just need to leave him alone and get off of his back."

She totally took his side. We wanted so much to leave the business. We were in the middle. If we quit, the business would fall apart. Kyle would win and Mom would not have the money she needed to take care of herself. We were putting money back for her so she would never have to go into a nursing home. She seemed to forget all the things we did for her. He would run through her money and kick her out in the cold. We never took one penny that belonged to her or Kyle. He was the one buying boats, trucks and new cars. That was their business. We only put money in her account when she asked us to. She always had an account that she kept for herself, because she knew that he would ask her for every penny she had. He would tell her that if something happened to her he would not have any money. He couldn't even stay in the house. "I have nothing." he would say to her. She would fall for all the poor me stories. He was getting a pension and anything he wanted from her salary. He had the camp, boats, all kinds of tools and trailers. She didn't even know what all he had stuffed in the barn behind the day care. He had it locked and it was all his. He had his own playground.

Mom cried for about a month and yelled at us for weeks. She would start the guilt trip on us. How could you do this to me? We stayed away from her and didn't tell her anything that was going on in the center. It was killing her not to know what was happening. She only had Kyle to talk to and get information about the nursery. We kept our distance. She wanted to see her grandchildren. She wanted us to come to lunch. She missed us. I know it was a bad time for her. It was such a put down for us. She had truly hurt both of us and we didn't want to be around her or him. Christmas was coming up and we didn't know how to get around the family event. Mom would call and ask us what size one

of the kids wore. She would make excuses for us to come by her
house. We would see him, but ignore him. This went on until the
first of December. I remember hating to go to her house for
Christmas. Kyle had told Sarah and Ron about the problem and
they were very cold to us. We all bought gifts for each other but
they were not the same kind we always got. Ron and his wife made
our gifts. Sarah bought us towels. Usually we made a list and
chose something on the list that we really wanted. There was a
rotten smell in the air. Everyone was on pins and needles. From
that time on we never had the same type of Christmas' together.
Kyle was out to get us. He watched every move we made.

Mom wanted one of us on her side. She would tell me things
Janice would say about me and tell Janice that I said this or that
about her. She would twist everything around and make it sound
like we were turning against each other. We couldn't believe that
she would do anything to tear us apart so we believed her. I would
go over to see her in the mornings and take my dog. Mom loved
Benji, my dog. She would tell me that Janice was sick and said
that I needed to step up to the plate and do a better job of working
in the office. I didn't help her with paper work. She would be sick
because she had to work so long at home. I would then defend
myself that I worked from 8:30 till closing with two kids. We never
bothered to check with each other about the gossip. It wasn't until
I quit the daycare that we finally figured out what she was doing.
She was becoming just like Kyle. I hated to be at the house, yet my
kids wanted to see their grandmother.

As time went on, I think she started to face reality. She knew
that she couldn't take care of her business. She also didn't trust
Kyle with her business. He was revealing more and more of his
hateful self. We told her not to believe things he was saying about
the daycare. After all we had been there for fifteen years and we
were more than qualified to run the business.

Matthew 23:23
   *You have neglected the more important matters of the
law – justice, mercy, and faithfulness.*

What's in the Will?

She would tell me that she wanted me to have this or that. She wanted the boys to have things and I would just say, "Okay, Mom." I knew that once she was gone we would never have a say over her things. She was always preoccupied with her diamonds. She would say "How will you divide these when I am gone." We tried to explain that anything she wanted us to have would have to be written in her will. She never listed anything she talked about. She never lost interest in her money. She was a business woman to the very end.

One day, when we were sitting at her kitchen table, Mom said she wanted to see her will. She said she wanted to make sure that Kyle was left with plenty, but she wanted us girls to have her personal things. Each quarter we met with the accountant to discuss the business. We always took Mom when she felt like going. Mom went with us to the CPA and we discussed making the business a corporation. We had talked about it before, but she did not really understand the whole process. We let her talk to the CPA and ask any questions she wanted. He explained that if the business was ever in trouble we would lose the business, but no one could touch our personal assets. She then began to ask questions about her will. With the encouragement from the CPA, she decided to look at her will and see what she had written. She was pumped to go and see the lawyer. It was not our idea. She set a day and all three of us went to the lawyer so she could read her will. She saw for herself that if she died that Kyle was in good shape as far as the house and joint belongings. She then went over all the daycare business with the lawyer and said that she wanted us to have the business. She even made us power of attorney. She wanted to make sure that the buildings were in our name and that if something happened to her that we would be the ones to make the decisions about her life. Both of us were shocked. I think something opened her eyes. She knew that he was not there for her best interest. She never told him that we were on the deeds and she never told him that we were power of attorneys.

He was beginning to take over her whole life. She was getting weaker and needed a walker to walk. When the care giver left for the day, she had to depend on him for help in cooking and doing simple household chores. We would bring her food or clothes whenever we could. Just bringing the kids made her smile. Whenever we went out of town we would leave the boys with them. They would run errands for her and help her walk to the bathroom and the family room. She loved to see her grandchildren come in the door. That was the best part of her day. She loved my boys and they loved her.

We encouraged her to go to the lake as much as possible. They had a ramp put on the front of the lake house so she could walk right into the bedroom. She and her sister along with Kyle and my uncle would go down during the week and fish. Mom was happy having her sister with her. Being at the lake helped keep Kyle busy and out of her face. Christeen and Mom were best friends. They loved to watch TV, fish and take long naps in the afternoon. Mom loved to cook so they would stop at the grocery on the way to the lake and grab some stakes and potatoes. Mom loved fresh vegetables and always looked for peaches or corn at roadside stands on the way to the river. She always wrote stories in her diary about how many fish she caught or what she cooked at the lake.

Mom always ended her entries with,
I had a wonderful time.

However, Mom was becoming more and more depressed. She didn't want to go anywhere or do anything. She was always afraid that she couldn't get around or do things on her own. She was hospitalized several times for congestive heart failure. Each time the doctor would tell her that she needed to rest when she got tired and reminded her that she was not the same person she was ten years ago. Mom never got it. She was always looking for a new pill that would save her or make her brand new. She would go to her family doctor with new symptoms almost monthly. He was her distant cousin and he would always encourage her and tell her to go fishing and be glad that she was doing so well. He would supply her with a new water pill or nerve pill to calm her nerves. He encouraged her to rest and spend time with her family. She had already beaten the odds for someone her age. Her heart doctor was in awe of her progress considering the condition of her heart.

He would do anything to keep her going as long as she wouldn't give up. He put a pacemaker in her chest and it lasted for five years or more.

We often told Mom that the Lord was not finished with her. She would pray asking God to heal her so she could spend more time with her grandchildren. She enjoyed her family and was still a witness to nurses and home health care that came to her house.

God wants us to stand firm in him. This Mom was sure to do until the day she died.

Ephesians 6:10-11

Finally, be strong in the Lord and in His mighty power. Put on the full armor of God so that you can take your stand against the devil's schemes.

Last Few Weeks of Freedom

Mom wanted so much for us all to be one big happy family. It was never happy and will never be that way. Kyle had so much hate for us and for Mom's affection for us.

We wanted to take her to lunch and we encouraged her to get a motorized wheelchair so she could go shopping and out to lunch. She called in a company and ordered one right away. Kyle was so bossy about it that he convinced her that there was no way she could drive it. He would not leave her alone to try by herself. He kept telling her that she was going to tip it over and run into the wall. It was impossible to sit still and watch her take that abuse.

So many times, we had to keep quite when he was on his soapbox about how she was doing something wrong. We encouraged her to try another motorized chair and she did. It was harder to steer and right away she gave up. He convinced her to send them back and as far as I know they were never used inside or outside the house. He did not want her to have any freedom. He liked her being shut inside the house. He would answer the phone and tell us she was lying down and never tell her we called. I so wished we could have had her alone with us for one last shopping trip. That was the only time she gave us any mother-daughter time. I read in her journal about shopping trips with Janice and how she respected her opinion on certain pieces of clothing. She always listened to Janice. She secretly knew that Janice was on the ball about things and she wouldn't steer her wrong. Mom would never admit it to Janice, but she did take her advice. Me, on the other hand, I couldn't do anything right. She had a thing going on with me – my hair and weight. She never cared if she hurt my feelings. She would just say, "That makes you look fat. Don't wear it anymore." I got use to the criticism over the years and learned that I would never please her so I never talked back.

One of our last trips together was at a country store in Indiana.

We pushed her in the wheelchair and she told us to pick out anything we wanted. She said, "I'll buy it." We both got vegetables, candy and little rock figures for our front yard. It was fall and we went to the bakery and bought fresh pies and pumpkins. The next time Janice and I went over to the country store, I had to cry. I can still see her looking around and saying pick out anything you two want. I am going to pay for it. What a day it was.

I got used to the criticism Mom was always giving me. I almost expected it. If I had known the Bible, I would have read that Jesus teaches about criticizing others.

Matthew 7:1,2
Do not judge, or you too will be judged. For in the same way you judge others, you will be judged, and with the measure you use, it will be measured to you.

The Daycare Takes a Turn

Mom continued to fail in her health. She was rushed to the hospital again with breathing problems. She was sent home after a short stay. She was given an IV of diuretics and put on a monitor for twenty-four hours. We knew that Mom was failing, but we would never act like we were worried. The doctor ordered a home health nurse to come to the house and monitor her blood pressure and pulse. She would check up on her mobility and keep her moving around the house. Soon Mom was looking forward to her visit. I think she gave her confidence that she was lacking from Kyle. The second nurse became a sounding board for Mom. I think Mom must have shared all of her family concerns with this lady. I met her recently and she was asking me about my stepfather, and in the next breath she was asking me about other members of his family. Mom loved people and in her last days she missed having parties and entertaining.

Janice and I were becoming very discouraged with the business. We were finding fault with each other and the employees were all getting burnt out with their jobs. The hyper kids, parents and paperwork put us all on edge. Rules and regulations were so tough. We were seeing a turnover of employees. This was never a problem with our center. New employees were stealing, trying to get fired and faking injuries to get money or unemployment. We had so much to contend with. Everything had to be in writing. It was getting impossible to run the business and be a mother. We were both discouraged. We wanted out. But how? Each morning as we arrived, we had employees lined up in front of the office to share some sort of problem with us. Teachers were not showing up on time. New teachers were refusing to go to other classrooms to help when needed. Everyone wanted time off. Mondays were always hard because everyone wanted long weekends. We would have to take classes until we could get teachers moved around or call in substitutes. The breaks were never the same. We started at nine arranging breaks for the afternoons. On top of all of this, we had to deal with mom and Kyle.

One day, as I was working in the office, a lady came in and gave me her card and asked if we would ever consider selling the business. A light bulb went off in my head. Wow! That's it! We could sell the business and do something we really wanted to do. I took her card and called Janice at home. She called the lady and we went to talk to the realtor.

She introduced us to a partner who would be helping her, and they told us that they wanted seven percent of the asking price. Janice and I talked it over and said it wouldn't even pay us to sell with that amount of money going to the realtor. We talked to Mom and she was highly disappointed that we would even consider selling her business. She would go back into her speech that, "if I was just ten years younger I could take it back and make all kinds of money. What's wrong with you girls? I should have never left the daycare." Here we go again. We had heard that speech over and over at least one hundred times before. I couldn't go on working at the center like it was. Kindergarten was phasing out and we didn't have enough kids for two classes. I was working at the main office with Janice and we were getting on each other's nerves. The employees were not seeing me as an equal director, because they were used to going to her with their problems. We did things so differently. Mom didn't help with her telling each one of us different stories about the other. I knew it was time to move on.

I talked to Richard and we both agreed that maybe I should look for something else. I had seen a bookmobile pass me every morning on my way to work. I got the idea that maybe I could open up a learning center for children and tell stories or do crafts. We looked for a building and we found more than we bargained for. A realtor found us a new church that was vacant with one hundred thirty two seats.

I had a meeting with one of the actors at a local theatre, and he convinced me to open a children's theatre. We borrowed money from Richard's aunt and father. We opened the theater in August of 1996. This caused a big rift in the family.

Janice said I deserted her and Mom was also upset. I felt so guilty that I ended up in therapy. I cried day and night. My therapist encouraged me to continue to follow my dream. My sister had a nervous breakdown, and Mom was just thinking about the money she would be losing. She didn't realize that we could not continue to work with the stress the business and the family problems were putting on us.

Janice tried to hire a director, but it didn't work. The girls hated her. We then tried to move a teacher into a director's position. This didn't work. We had several offers and at one time, we thought we had the daycare sold. Weeks later, we learned that the buyer didn't have the money, and so we were back to square one.

Each month was getting harder on us as partners and sisters. We were not talking, but accusing each other of everything. Mom was not helping at all. She was so mad and Kyle was fueling her on. He continued his spy work every morning and kept her informed on the activities of the day. As always he made everything sound like a tragedy. I was praying that we could sell the place. I was also working on my new place, trying to contact schools and daycares to inform them about the theatre. I worked day and night. When I did go home I had to listen to Mom. She would call me and cry and tell me how ungrateful I was. Then, she would throw in the fact that I wouldn't let the boys stay with her. I was a mess. My marriage almost fell apart. I was never at home. I missed my sister and yet I just couldn't go back to work. I had had enough of the daycare and the whole family. Christmas 1997 I did not want to go home. I was still in therapy and my therapist suggested that I not go to Mom's for Christmas. I really wanted not to buy any gifts or just send them and stay at my house. I thought I could send the family and I could stay home. I cried for weeks. I finally gave in and went to Mom's house for Christmas. I was in knots inside. Everything I said or did was judged by my Mom. We all took pictures not with each other, but with our own families. As soon as the gifts were open we headed back home.

I know it was really hard on my sister. It just seemed that no one would make a decision about the daycare. I just had to leave. I was now working more hours than ever, writing shows, writing music, and making sets. I also had to advertise in the afternoons going from school to school, calling daycares and sending out mail to the neighbors. I had shows on Saturday and birthday parties in the theater rainforest room. We spent every waking minute in the theater. My sister, on the other hand, was still in the battlefield fighting the masses. Finally we had a savior. She stepped in and became the director and let my sister off the hook. After a year of directing, she found a buyer and we all agreed that it was time to move on. The day we signed the papers to sell the daycare, was the happiest day of our lives. For once we could go home and talk to Mom without talking about the daycare.

Mom was getting weaker, but she lost all hope the next year when her baby sister Christeen died. In her diary she writes, *"I lost my best friend. I'll never be the same."* I really don't think she ever was the same. Her caregiver that had worked for her for over thirty years had to quit to take care of her sister, who was dying in a nearby hospital. Mom had no one to take care of her during the day. Now she had to rely on Kyle. He was bound to the house day and night. He hated being there and she hated him taking care of her. She told us that he was always mistreating her and yelling at her. If she missed the pot or misplaced something he would get mad and push her. She said he was cussing and making her life miserable. She couldn't trust him anymore. She told us that he got very angry at times and would throw things across the room and cuss at her. "You just don't know what I go through. Night and day he makes life miserable. I am so big and he can't get me up if I fall. He pushes around on me, trying to get me up in the bed. He hates to get my clothes ready so I can try to give myself a bath. I just hate for him to have to wash me and take care of me. If I was well, and a lot younger I would get a divorce. I simply hate him."

We talked it over and decided that Mom needed someone to come into the house and take care of her. She needed someone to cook for her and help her get her bath. I found a woman who lived close by and told Mom about her. Mom started figuring up the cost and went berserk. Kyle wasn't much better. How could we suggest such thing? It was going to eat up all of her money. We explained to Mom that we would pay for the extra help. She wouldn't hear of that. After all, she still had lots of money in her account. Mom fussed and fumed for days. When the lady came for the interview Mom was very hateful to her. It was all about the money. We tried to talk to her without Kyle, but he had already poisoned her about the idea. Mom had plenty of money coming in from her Social

Security. Every option we suggested, she would shoot down. We knew she didn't have long to live, but we never would have told her that. We always tried to be upbeat and encourage her. Still, she would not consider giving money to someone to come into the house for a few hours a day to help her cook and bathe. Instead, she would call me at work to come and give her a bath and help her have a bowl movement. I would drop everything I was doing at my theater and run into her house to give her a suppository and wash her hair. It didn't matter what I had going on, her needs came first. I remember once when I had surgery, she came to my house to stay with me. I waited on her hand and foot that day. I had to get her medicine, find her purse, and cook up something for lunch. She never even considered that I had my tummy cut open and could hardly move up and down. It was always about her.

Kyle was behind the money thing, too. He didn't want someone in the house watching him and asking questions. He also hated spending money he might get after her death. Instead, they bought new carpet for the family room, kitchen and hall. Mom cashed in her life insurance and bought several new things. He didn't even know what she had done with all her money from the daycare. I can't remember all her purchases. I do know he wanted a new boat. We asked her what she was thinking. "You know, if something happens to you then he will have a new woman in here. Are you going to fix this old house up for another woman? You could use this money to hire someone to take care of you."

It wasn't long before her sister Evelyn got real sick and needed to have some surgery. Janice and I went to Indiana and brought her to Louisville to the doctor. She stayed at my house because Mom couldn't take care of her. Mom was really mad that I kept her with me and refused to come to my house. Mom demanded that I bring her to her house. I did and they were so glad to be together. Kyle slept on the couch and the two sisters slept together in the bed. Evelyn got a little blood on the sheets and Kyle got upset. I went over and changed the sheets, changed her bandage and tried to keep peace. Mom was insistent that she go home. She called her son and asked him to pick her up. I know that Kyle was behind this.

Evelyn had more visits with the doctor, and Mom again wanted her sister to come over and spend the two days with her. At this point Kyle was very upset. Mom knew that her sister needed a care giver and considered having someone come to her house and take care of both of them. We knew that this would be an excellent idea, but I could see fireworks coming from Kyle's eyes. I can't remember if someone came for a week, but I do remember that someone came for just a few hours to help with cooking while Evelyn was there. Mom was always eager to see her sisters and always wanted to be with both of them whenever she could. This time she understood that she was not able to take care of Evelyn. I had to come over to her house and bathe both of them and fix their hair. I tried to make everything easy on everyone. Mom was always jealous of my aunt and me. She would ask me, "Why are you so crazy about Evelyn?" She didn't understand that she was always kind to me and interested in what I was telling her about my life. She was truly a kind person. She loved me very much. She knew how to show her love. She would ask me questions about my life. She was proud of me. She wasn't critical of me. I was always perfect in her eyes.

My uncle Jay was visiting the house when I brought Evelyn to spend the night at Mom's for her last visit and check up at the doctor's office. Janice and I went to Indiana to get her and brought her straight to Mom's house just as Mom had instructed us to do. Evelyn insisted that she sleep on the pull out couch and Kyle stay in bed with Mom. We all agreed.

Mom looked at Kyle and said, "Go upstairs and get some extra sheets out of Linda's old bedroom dresser."

Kyle gave her looks that would kill. He stomped up the stairs while yelling, "I don't know where to look."

He came down the steps and threw the sheets at me and Janice who were sitting on the love seat next to the pull-out couch. I could see fire in his eyes. I remember saying to Janice. "I bet Mom is telling us the truth. He must blow up all the time like this. Poor Evelyn! I am sure he won't want to take care of her or help her to the bathroom. I'll try to get over there early tomorrow to make sure they are both up and dressed. Mom wants me to wash their hair." Janice said she would cook them something for lunch, and so we agreed to meet back over at Mom's house early the next morning. My uncle also came back for lunch and to visit with Evelyn. Someone bought over donuts for breakfast and Janice was busy making lunch as I started combing Evelyn's hair getting her ready to take to the doctor. Mom was in her wheelchair and was trying to drink her coffee.

Kyle came through the room and was mad that he couldn't walk through the kitchen because Mom's chair was in his way. He pushed her into the table as hard as he could and said, "Scoot up at the table. You're getting food all over the place."

She replied, "That's as far as I can get to the table. Give me a chance, and I will get out of your way."

Poor thing she was trying to move her feet and she was stuck way up under the table where he pushed her.

I then replied, "Sometimes I don't like the way you talk to my mother."

He got in my face and yelled, "You can just leave this house. *Now*!"

I looked at him and said, "I won't leave as long as my mother is living here."

At this point, Janice jumped in and told him that he was not going to talk to me that way. "We are here to take care of our mother and she is sick of you. We all are!"

I stared back at him and said, "We know how you have been treating her."

He, of course, started yelling and denied everything. Mom got so upset with us. She just knew that we would all end up on the floor in a big fist fight.

My uncle in the family room only got in on the last part of the argument and started taking up for Kyle. "I can't believe how those girls are talking to you." Kyle mumbled something and they both went out on the deck badmouthing us. Mom was crying and blaming us for causing trouble.

I told her I was only taking up for her. "Mom, why do you allow him to treat you that way?"

She screams back at us, "I don't have a choice. He'll probably leave now. Why didn't you keep your big mouth shut?"

"Mom! What are you saying? Do you want me to leave?"

"No, but why did you have to go and tell him what I said?"

I replied, "Fine, I'll take care of Evelyn's hair and I will take her to the doctor and you won't have to worry about me coming back here to cause you trouble."

Evelyn was crying by now and Janice was still mouthing off about Kyle. We finished our task of fixing hair and lunch and we both left. I brought Evelyn back to Mom's and then left without a word.

That night, when I got home, Mom called me and I could tell that she and Kyle had been talking. He must have given her an earful about us girls. Mom was still very upset with me. She said her biggest mistake was not making me move in with my dad when I was little. She really hurt me this time. It was a hurt that I will never forget. She could have just said, "I hate you and wish you were never born." Why would she say this after all I had done for her?

This is what she would always come back with when we talked back to her. "How could you talk to me like that after all I have done for you?" I should have used her line. Ha!

I tried to stay away from her for the next few weeks. I was so hurt. She called my cousin to come and get my aunt and he was wondering what the deal was. She was supposed to stay till the end of the weekend. I told him the whole story about Kyle and his hateful actions. I explained, "He really doesn't want your Mom there. She is so upset with the whole deal. Maybe it would be a good idea to keep her away from the house right now."

He knew what Kyle was like. None of Mom's family liked him. They were really upset when she married him. My Aunt Christeen would put up with him so she and Mom could go to the lake together. Teen had told us how he bossed her around on the boat. She said they were always arguing. He fussed about everything. We knew she was telling us the truth. After all, we had put up with him for years. When we were old enough to use the boat or camper, he would never let us behind the wheel. It would have been nice to have the camper and share a trip with my sister and her family. We knew that this was never going to happen. He would not let us near any of his toys. We did go down to the lake before Mom died and wash all of her curtains, blankets, windows, and also we mowed the grass. We cleaned the whole camp for her. Kyle was so upset. He thought that we were trying to get the camp in our names. He said, "What is the deal behind all of this? I guess they are going to try to take the lake."

Kyle was always suspicious of everything we did. If we did

anything for either of them he would tell Mom that we were doing it for some motive. He never said thank you, but complained that someone had fished with his rod and reel and had them all tangled up together. What a joke! We didn't have time for fishing. We knew that mom liked to go down there and she wasn't able to clean it anymore, so we did it for her. Thankfully she did make it one more time. She got to see it all cleaned up and was very proud.

Psalm 10:2-4

In his arrogance the wicked man hunts down the weak who are caught in the schemes he devises. He boasts of the carvings of his heart; he blesses the greedy and reviles the Lord. In his pride the wicked does not seek Him; in all his thoughts there is no room for God.

The Last Days

It was February, 2003. We had just celebrated her birthday in January and she was 85. We all went to Mom's house to eat pizza and cake. We got her sweaters and I bought her a little tape recorder so she could finish her book for me. She said she would like to see it all finished before something happened to her. Janice now had a new grandbaby born in December, and Mom loved being with him. She would just look at him and say, "Isn't he a doll?" On Sunday, we took her out to eat to her favorite place in Shelbyville. We all acted like that perfect family one more time.

I got a phone call once again from my sister. It was like many calls we had received before. "Sis, Mom is having problems breathing and I am over here with her. We put a call into the doctor, but I think we should just take her on to the hospital."

I replied, "Well she hasn't been feeling good for a long time now so maybe you should see what is going on. Do I need to come?"

"No, the weather is so bad, we have called the EMS and I'll call you when we get to the hospital."

There was a devastating ice storm that night. The weather men were asking people to stay off the roads. My children were watching to see if school would be open the next day. Later that night she called back and told me that they could not take her to the hospital we always went to.

"We had to take her to the nearest hospital." Janice announced.

I replied, "Her doctor doesn't go to that hospital does he?"

"No, but a heart specialist will come by and take care of her."

"Okay! Do I need to come up?"

"No, she is sleeping now and we are still in the emergency room. Kyle is here and he said he was going to stay with her until they get her a room. You can come up in the morning. Her heart is very weak. I've been watching the monitor. The doctor will be by soon and I'll leave after he tells us what is going on."

Janice recalls, "That night in the small emergency room Mom told me to take her rings off and keep them. Her hands were swollen and I worked hard to twist them off."

Kyle came into the room and saw Janice trying to take off her rings. He said, "She can keep them on her."

Mom looked at him and said, "No, I want Janice to take them."

Janice didn't even look up and put the rings in her purse. She reported, "I could tell that Kyle wasn't happy with Mom's decision."

Janice called me early the next day at my theatre. "It doesn't look good. She had a heart attack and her pacemaker took over and shocked her. It scared her to death. We were right to get her here right away. See if you can get things together at work and then come up. I'll meet you at the hospital."

"Is Kyle there" I asked?

"No, he went home to get some rest."

"Okay, I'll be there as soon as the show gets started."

I ushered all the kids into the theatre and started the show and quickly went to the hospital to see about Mom. They had her on a heart monitor. My uncle and his son were there and I walked in to see her. She looked up at me and said, "Linda, this is it. The doctor told me this morning that there wasn't much he could do. I am going to die."

I looked at my uncle and cousin and both of them started to cry. My cousin walked out of the room, and Mom looked at my uncle and said, "Is there anything you want me to tell Teen when I get to heaven?"

He looked at her with tears in his eyes and said, "No, I'll tell her myself."

Mom was crying and staring into space. I took her hand and hugged her.

"Mom, I am jealous of you. You're going to get to heaven before me."

Mom replied, "Yes, but I am scared. I don't know what to expect."

I sat down on her bed and said, "How can you say that? You have been a Christian all your life. You know God will take care of you. Where is your faith? Besides, we don't even know what the doctor has in store for you. You have always bounced back. Let's just take this thing one day at a time." I could tell that her mind was far away. She must have had a million things on her mind. I told her that I loved her and I don't remember if we prayed, but I do remember that she calmed down a little and then started vomiting. The nurse came in and saw the heart rate and said we needed to get her upstairs in the intensive care unit. Mom looked like she had slipped into a coma and the nurse called for help and we pushed the bed down the hall and into the elevator up to the unit. They were just opening the unit and the nurse and I were the only people up there. I stayed with Mom and wiped her head as the nurse called for help and started a new IV. She was also calling for her doctor. Mom was not aware of what was going on around her. She had her eyes open and I thought for sure she was gone. The nurse asked me if I could stay with her until she could get some nurses up there to help her and I agreed. I could see that she was still breathing and I kept calling "MOM!" She looked at me and then from nowhere several nurses were there working with her.

The nurse took me to the side and said, "Does she have a living will?"

I said, "No! Should I call the family?"

"Yes," she replied, "that would be a good idea."

I slipped out and called Janice. "Janice, mom is going into some kind of shock and they want the family to come in right away. You can call Kyle if you want. I am going back into the unit and sit with her. You don't have to call back. Just come to the second floor and walk back into her room."

Janice called Kyle and we all met in the unit with the nurse. She asked what we wanted to do if she needed to be shocked back to life.

Kyle immediately spoke up and said, "She has a pacemaker. What will that do?"

The nurse said it would keep her going and keep shocking her.

He said, "Well, I don't think she would want to stay alive on a respirator."

We looked at him and agreed. He had no idea we were the ones who were supposed to make that decision. We were very respectful to him. We let him stay in the room and kept our distance.

Later that night, Mom seemed to come around. The doctors

ordered medicine to regulate her heart and medicine to help calm
her down. She was conscious later that night and we were able to
talk to her. We tried to explain what was going on with her, but
she was trying to pull out her IVs and acted like she was not
coherent. We waited in the waiting room all night long and took
turns going back to see her. She made it through the night and the
next day she was looking around and talking to us. Feeling that
she was now out of the woods, I went home and got some sleep.

Later that night I went back up to the hospital and the whole
family along with Kyle's brothers was there. It looked like Kyle
and his kids and family were having a party. They stayed until
visiting hours were over and then Kyle's kids stayed through the
night with Janice and me. Mom had a good night's sleep, in and
out of consciousness.

When she was awake, she was confused and wanted to know
what was going on. It seemed like we were telling her the same
things over and over again. We now had to share our time in her
room with Ron and Sarah. It snowed that night and we all stayed
up looking out the window watching each little snowflake fall to
the top of the building.

Ron took Kyle home for some rest and all of us girls stayed
there on watch. As we slept in the waiting room, we would wake
up and check the clock and go into the room to check on Mom's
progress. You could see her heart rate on the monitor and see that
her breaths were very shallow. She rested most of the night.

When Mom was awake, we would hold her hand and talk to
her. She was very tired, but seemed content that we were there
with her. Once she was quiet and sleeping, we all went to
breakfast.

When Kyle returned, we left to go home and get some rest so
we could return for the evening. Ron, Kyle, and Sarah were
already there when Richard and I walked into the waiting room.
Janice, her husband and children were behind us as we took our
places to wait for our turns to go into the room to visit.

Ron was always loud. He took over and told us everything that
happened while we were gone. He gave us a doctor's report and
told us about the visitors who had floated in and out of the waiting
room. Once again Kyle's brothers and sisters-in-laws were back
partying in the corner with Ron and now his kids and wife. The

loud laughing and talking was getting on my last nerve. Other people were there with their loved ones and they were also put out with the group. Janice and I decided to send everyone home and stay there by ourselves. Mom's oldest grandson C.T. was home and he stayed with us for awhile. Mom loved seeing him. Kyle of course would not go home at the end of visiting hours. He was determined to stay with us. He fell asleep in the lounge chair and I took the couch.

About 2:00, Janice and C.T. left to go home and I went in to stay with Mom. I slept in the chair next to her bed. She woke up and was talking out of her head. She kept talking about the daycare and the cots. "Who's staying with the kids over there?"

I tried to answer her questions without getting her upset. Then she started asking me where she was. I would tell her the name of the hospital and she would say this isn't the hospital where I go.

I would explain that we had to take her here because of the ice storm. She said, "No, I don't believe you. I haven't even seen my doctor. Why doesn't doctor Lynhart come to see me?"

I tried to explain that he doesn't come to this hospital, but he is keeping in touch with the other doctors. She tried to get out of the bed and look through the window into the nurses' station.

"Look," she said, "They are all foreign people in there." Sure enough, all of her doctors and nurses were not of American decent. I said, "Yes, Mom, but they are all here to take care of you. You're in the hospital."

She didn't believe me. She started yelling at me saying, "Where have you girls put me?" I tried to explain that she was in the hospital close to our house and that she was in the intensive care unit to monitor her heart.

She said, "I know what you are doing. Kyle warned me about you girls. He told me you two would put me away somewhere so you could get my money and now I see what he meant."

"What! I can't believe you would think that we would put you away somewhere."

"Look, I'll call the nurse in here and she can tell you."

She grabbed my hand and screamed, "Leave them alone. They'll come in here and take me away. They'll give me poison. They are all foreigners and want to kill me."

"Mom, lie down and don't say such silly things. You are in the hospital and these are nurses taking care of you."

She rose up out of the bed and grabbed at her arm. "Come on now, help me get out of here."

She was wild. "I should have listened to Kyle. He was telling me the truth. What have you done with Kyle?"

I couldn't believe her. I called the nurse when she wasn't looking and she tried to keep her in the bed and tell her that she was in the May's Hospital. She shook her head and rolled her eyes. She even tried to hit the nurse. Then she tried to hit me. I asked the nurse if she was on some kind of medicine that was causing her to go crazy. She said that she thought that her oxygen level was low and she thought that it was causing her to be forgetful. She left the room and came back to check her oxygen. Then she gave her some sleeping pill, but she seemed to be worse.

She was pulling on the covers and trying to get up. She was very angry with us girls. She kept saying, "Kyle was right. He knows what you two are up to. How could you do this to me? I have raised you two girls all by myself and given you everything and look what you do to me? You put me in this place all locked up with these foreign people."

I was so worn out trying to keep her calm and explain to her that she wasn't locked up. I told her I loved her and she said it was too late for that kind of thing.

"If you really loved me you would take me out of this prison."

It was now about 5:30 in the morning and I couldn't take it anymore. I slipped out of the room and called Janice. I told her that Kyle had filled her head with some kind of information about us putting her in a foreign prison. She asked me where Kyle was. I said, "He's here, but I don't want to wake him up and get him involved. I think I would belt him one right now. He has been filling her head with negative things about us. You need to get up here."

Janice agreed and she and her son came as soon as they could. Kyle remained sleeping in the chair. Mom calmed down when she saw her grandson, but she was still saying things that didn't make sense. At the 6:00 shift change I was hoping that she would get an American nurse.

As we sit in her room with her, trying to keep her still and bring her back to reality, a new nurse came in and said, "Mrs.

Violet, my name is Shoo Ti and I will be your nurse today." I couldn't believe what I was seeing.

Mom looked at me and said, "See, another foreigner. If you love me, you would get me out of here."

I had to laugh. I looked at Janice and C.T. and we all shook our heads. Soon Kyle was poking his nose into the room and she was asking him to take her out of the room. He said he would when she got better. The nurse suggested some new medicine and called the doctor to get his okay. Then she gave her the pill and she went off to sleep. What a long night! I left after C.T., Janice and I ate breakfast. I was worried about her but she had a good day, and the doctor said he wanted to move her into a regular room with a heart monitor. That night when I went to visit her she was sitting up and eating supper. Kyle was sitting there and I told him to go eat supper and I would stay with her.

While we were alone, I asked her if she remembered what she had said to me. She said, "You must be crazy. I don't remember any of that. I just know that I have been dead tired today."

I wanted to say, "You should be! You put me through hell last night."

Then she said, "I can't wait until the doctor lets me go home." I tried to explain to her that it might be awhile. I could see that she had no idea that she was still not out of the woods. She was worried about her hair and asking about the boys so I knew that she was back to her old self. She slept well that night and we all went home to rest, except Kyle.

The next day, we walked into her room and there was stillness about everyone sitting there. Sarah, Kyle, and Janice were watching a nurse give Mom medicine in her IV. Janice explained that she had had another heart attack, and her pacemaker had shocked her back to life. When the nurse left, she told me all about it. She said it was horrible." I just can't explain what pain I went through. They are calling the doctor now."

I stood there holding her hand and wiped her hair away from her forehead.

"Mom, everything will be alright. Thank God you had that pacemaker. Maybe they will get your medicine regulated and everything will be better."

She replied, "I hope so. I want to go home, but I can't go home with this thing acting up."

She thought that her pacemaker was broken. There was no
need in telling her that her heart was stopping and that she was
going into cardiac arrest. We had to keep her spirits up. The doctor
came in and talked to the whole family outside of her room. He
explained that he was going to put her back in the ICU unit and
give her oxygen. "We'll watch her for awhile and see how low her
pulse goes."

Mom was moved into the ICU unit, and Sarah, Janice and I
spent the night and sent Kyle home for some rest. We each took a
couch in the waiting room. I woke up and saw that Sarah was
gone. I walked back into Mom's room and Sarah was sitting there
watching her breathe. We held on to each other, and at that point I
realized that Mom was the only one who had ever cared about her.
She truly loved Mom. It was snowing again and we talked about
the lack of cars in the parking lot. The silence of the night was
grim as we took deep breaths when she would stop breathing for a
second. We both knew it was just a matter of time, but neither one
of us would say it. Mom slept through the night and the nurses
never left her alone. They offered us coffee and cokes. We walked
back into the waiting room and Janice lifted her head up to see if
we were sleeping. We laughed and told her she was fine and we all
confessed that we were exhausted from the events of the week.

The next twenty-four hours were quiet. My cousins came up to
see her but she didn't know they were even there. The doctor had
sedated her so much that she was in a deep sleep giving her heart
much needed rest. She remained in the unit for three days and
then they let up on the medicine and she became alert. Her heart
was still weak, but she had not had a MI in the days she spent in
the cardiac unit. The doctor moved her back to a regular room with
a heart monitor. He talked to the family doctor and said that there
wasn't anything more they could do for her. He explained that it
would be a blessing if she just went in her sleep. He said the
pacemaker was shocking her and it would only get worse as her
heart slowed down. He wanted to remove the pacemaker. We all
agreed with him. That evening with Mom not even aware of what
was happening, he disconnected the pacemaker for good. She was
in good spirits the days following the event. We couldn't get over
her clear mind and how she laughed and wanted to see all the

grandchildren. We called the boys and they came up to the room and talked to her. She remarked on each one of their hair dos. All you boys need haircuts. You are just too pretty to let yourselves go like that. Her three grandsons were all in her bed and she loved it. We fed her some ice cream and I remember her asking if there was any more. She said the food was horrible and she wished she was home to eat some real food. That day my friend came to see her and while we were all visiting Sarah called and said that Kyle's doctor wanted him to go into the emergency room because of his blood pressure. Sarah said, "I am afraid he won't go. He said he didn't think it was necessary." Mom said that she thought that he was not taking his medicine and probably needed it refilled. My friend who was a nurse suggested that we should go see about him. We headed toward Mom's to take his blood pressure and to make sure he had taken his prescription to the drugstore. We opened the door and he was in his closet where he kept guns and personal items. He heard us come in and thought it was Sarah. When he saw it was us, he jumped up and ran into the other room with something in his hand. Just as quickly as he left he returned to question us.

"What are you doing here?" He screamed.

I replied, "We just wanted to see if you were alright. Lilly wants to take your blood pressure."

He was so uncomfortable with our being there. He shifted his weight from one foot to the other. "I don't need anyone to take my blood pressure. I'll be alright."

We encouraged him to go to the hospital like the doctor wanted. He said he would be fine and he wanted us to go back to the hospital with Mom. We left and it wasn't until later on that he decided to check himself into the hospital.

Mom was truly doing better now. She didn't need anyone to spend the night with her. They doubled her heart medicine and she rested quietly all day and all night. She didn't seem worried about Kyle. Sarah called and announced that her dad was in the hospital so Janice and I went to the emergency room to check on him. He acted so strange.

"Why are you all here?"

We told him we were worried about him and wanted to see what was going on. You could tell that he hated us being there.

When Sarah came down we left and went back upstairs to stay
with Mom.

Romans 2:9-11

*There will be trouble and distress for every human being
who does evil: first for the Jew, then for the Gentile; but
glory, honor and peace for everyone who does good: first for
the Jew, then for the Gentile. For God does not show
favoritism.*

Time is Running Out

They didn't keep him in the hospital, but he did go home and rest. While he was away they moved Mom into a step-up unit for therapy. She was on a regular diet and was tired of her stay in the hospital. Some days she was mean as a snake. She demanded that she have juice, then she said she wanted Coca-Cola. Janice was feeding her and I remember she jumped all over her because she didn't feed her something or get her something quick enough. She didn't really know what she wanted. Janice had tried everything to make her happy. Never had she said, "I am sorry" or "Thank you." With Kyle away we started staying with her more. When he got better he started coming up and taking over. He talked to all the nurses and wouldn't take our word on what was going on.

Mom knew something was not right. She said, "Why are they keeping me so long?" We said that she had to walk and do some exercises to get her strength back. She was smarter than that. She knew that they would not even let her up out of bed to go to the bathroom.

So she asked, "When are they going to start the exercises?"

"I guess when you get stronger." I replied.

Mom was beginning to feel better and she just knew that she would be going home. One day Janice started asking her what she was going to do when she got home.

"You know mom, you will need someone to help you."

"Kyle will take care of me," she replied.

Janice tried to tell her that Kyle was not well enough to take care of her. Then she said, "Mom, is there anything you want to say to us in case something happens to you?"

What a response she got from that question!

"How dare you talk to your mother like that? You think I am going to die don't you? How could you even say something to me like that knowing how sick I've been?"

Janice just shook her head. "Mom, you realize that you are still very sick and I just wondered if you needed to talk or something."

She just responded, "I wouldn't even think of saying something like that to my mother."

At this point, we knew that she was never going to accept the fact that she had a health problem. As Mom became more stable, she was going to be released to hospice. The doctor had mentioned it to us and we agreed that it would be a good idea.

One day, as we walked up to Mom's room, a nurse approached us and said someone from hospice wanted to talk to us. Kyle, Janice and I met with her in the lobby of the third floor. She told us that we needed to sign some papers. We let Kyle take charge as he always did. When we got to the part where she asked if she had a power of attorney, Kyle said no. She then said that she needed to establish one.

Janice and I looked at each other and I said, "Yes! We are."

Kyle's face got red, and he looked like he wanted to hit something. He got up from the meeting, and said, "Talk to them." He was really mad at us. This was something Mom did, and we agreed to sign the papers.

The nurse continued to tell us what to expect and had us sign a paper saying that if something was to happen at home, she would not be rushed back to the hospital. They would try to keep her as comfortable as possible with morphine. "We will get her a hospital bed and give you all the numbers you need to call in case something happens."

We agreed that it was the right thing to do, and then we went back into Mom's room. Kyle was not there. He came in later as we were leaving. He was mad at Mom and let her know how he felt.

He said, "From now on you two can stay with her and I will stay away."

That is just what happened. For the next week we each took turns staying with her at night. We turned her and helped her on and off of the bedside potty. We fed her and had long talks. She confessed that she knew what was wrong with Kyle.

"He's mad at me because you girls are power of attorney. I don't care. I would rather have you all up here anyways."

We waited on her hand and foot. Kyle would visit for a short time during the day and was sure to stay away from us. One day a minister from the hospital came to visit with the family. Sarah, Ron, Kyle, Janice and I were taken to a private room so he could pray with us. He asked us about the family and if we understood what was going to happen to her once she got home. We all cried and agreed that we understood about her health, but I really knew what was going to happen. Kyle was going to shut us out. We would never be a family again. Not the kind of family Mom thought we were. We had to save face with Mom. Whatever happened I had to be kind and nice. I was doing it for Mom.

The day came when the doctors released her to go home. They said her heart rate was very weak, but they couldn't give us any time line of when her death would take place. We ordered a hospital bed and it arrived before they let her out of the hospital. We needed someone to take care of her and cook for her. I called my friend that ran a senior home and she sent her husband out to talk to the family. Kyle didn't like the idea. We then found someone in the paper that would come in during the day and stay with her. We talked with her and she had plenty of experience. In reality, Kyle knew that she was so bad that he needed someone to help him take care of her. The night we brought her home I made dinner and fixed her tomato soup. She loved it. I remember she ate like she had never had food before in her life. I also made a chicken noodle dish with green beans for Kyle and lunch the next day. I even made a cake. Mom looked at me and said, "I wish my sister Evelyn had some of this soup. I wish she could be up here with me." I was so proud that for once in my life she liked what I had done for her. She told me she loved me and I did her dishes and went home.

The next day, Janice came over to get Mom's medicine lined out. Kyle sat down with her and they wrote and rewrote all the medicine that was supposed to be given to her in the morning, noon, and evening. He couldn't get the morphine thing right. She tried to explain that she didn't get it unless she was in pain. The new care giver was there and helped her turn in bed and go to the bedside potty. Mom didn't like her much, but she would have to get use to it. I met her at noon and realized that she had body odor so bad that I couldn't be in the same room with her. Gee! What were we going to do? Kyle didn't like her much either, but she was good to Mom and maybe we could address the body odor.

On Sunday after Mom had been home since Friday, we all gathered into the house to eat with her and spend some time as her family. Everyone was there except Ron and his family. After lunch, we cleared the dishes and Sarah and her family left the house. Janice and I stayed with Mom and I washed and dried her hair. It was a major task trying to pour water over her head as she laid it back to allow me to scrub and clean with real shampoo and not the fake stuff used in the hospital. This would be the first good shampoo she had had in months. Mom was in a good mood. She talked to us and Janice begins to go through her dresser drawers as we causally discussed the new caregiver and the hospital bed. Kyle meanwhile was watching the final basketball tournaments in the family room right outside the bedroom. We teased her about her ratty looking underwear and some old belts and scarves she hadn't worn in years. As we laughed Janice was throwing away unwanted items and cleaning out old memories that Mom was sure she had thrown away in years past. It was a good day. I had her all cleaned up and setting up with her hair fixed. We had bags and bags of things for the garbage. Mom looked at her jewelry box and wanted us to go through it. Kyle saw that we were close to his closet and he lost interest in the game and started listening in on our conversation. He informed us that the things in the closet were his.

Mom replied, "Yes, Kyle, we know that is your closet and no one is going to touch a thing of yours." We asked her about her jewelry and different pieces she had collected. We would look for her diamond bracelet, her expensive necklace Janice brought back from England, her diamond droplets. Nothing could be found.

Then she yelled at Kyle and said, "What have you done with my good jewelry?" He pretended that he didn't know what she was talking about. Mom was on the ball. She said, "You always hid my good jewelry when we go to the lake. Now what did you do with it?"

Kyle always acted dumb whenever he didn't want to answer a question. "It was in your jewelry box," he replied.

Mom told us to go into the bathroom and look on a nail behind the curtain. I did as she told me and found no jewelry. Mom continued, "You know who put it all up? I'll make him find it when you two leave. He has it hidden somewhere."

She had several chains of gold and silver. She had a diamond watch that she could not find for years and other diamond necklaces that were her pride and joy. We knew what she was talking about. It was Kyle. He wanted to make sure that no one got a thing out of her jewelry box, especially us. As the day went on, we had forgotten the conflict Mom and Kyle had about the jewelry and we gathered for the second meal and kissed her goodbye saying we would return tomorrow.

Mom was tired and was sleeping when we left.

That night I saw a peace come over Mom as she slept. God had taken away her pain with the help of the medications. She felt good knowing she had her hair styled, was bathed, had good food to eat, and was now safely surrounded by her family.

John 14:27

Peace I leave with you, My peace I give you. I do not give to you as the world gives. Do not let your hearts be troubled and do not be afraid.

Seven Long Days

The next day was Monday and Mom did not want to eat. The good thoughts of Sunday had disappeared and she was restless. Showing some signs of pain and running a temperature. She now had a cough and her breathing was very shallow. The cough was getting worse and she was not talking much.

The caregiver was trying her best to keep Mom cool with a wet washcloth, and at lunchtime, we came back to see her. She ate some, but still she was not up to having a lot of company. She asked us questions about our families, and was able to get in and out of bed to go to the bedside potty.

By Tuesday, she was still trying her best to hang in there. She ate some soup and drank little of nothing. Her breathing was worse and the look on her face showed pain and distress. We called the hospice nurse and she told us to give her some morphine. Later, the nurse called back and said she would try to stop by.

By 6:00 P.M. on Tuesday, we were all gathered around her bed to listen and try to talk to her. She was very much aware of her pain and that we were in the room. She talked to each one of us, but only in short sentences. Her mouth was dry and we tried to keep it wet with a cold cloth. Her temperature was getting higher and we addressed it with drugs as we were told. On Wednesday the nurse came by and told us that she was slipping in and out of consciousness. She gave us some suggestions on how to keep her comfortable and didn't say how long she could live, but guaranteed us that it wouldn't be long. Thursday was a horrible day for the whole family. Mom was now eating and drinking nothing. We would try to get her to drink, but she was slipping away right before our eyes. Her breathing was getting harder and the sound she made when she coughed was heart wrenching. We could take not another minute of the pain she was sharing with us. The drugs didn't seem to help. She was coughing harder and harder and each breath seemed like it was her last. Janice called the nurse on Friday and she said that she would suggest that we send her to the hospital by ambulance.

Kyle had a doctor's appointment on Friday. He returned home and was diagnosed with congestive heart failure and needed to be sent to the hospital right away. They wanted to draw the fluid off of his body. Sarah was concerned about his health and begged him to do as the doctor requested and go into the hospital. He refused. He was now having chest pains and we all jumped on him to seek professional help. We told him that we would call him if things got worse with Mom. We all waited about three more hours and then Kyle gave in and the EMS came to get Mom. All of us headed off to different hospitals for different reasons. Janice and I spent the night in the room with Mom. We couldn't sleep as we hashed over our life and watched her try to take in air. The nurses were concerned for us. They said we should leave the room from time to time. We walked out into the waiting room and called our husbands and children. We made some plans and explained that the time looked close. On Saturday as we waited our oldest cousin whom we rarely talked with came to spend time with us. He brought us fond memories that helped us to laugh and relive the good times. Mom was still hanging in there, but was no longer able to move or breathe on her own. She now had oxygen and was given a steady dose of pain medicine and sleeping pills. Her temperature was now 106 degrees. My two boys came by and as they spoke her name, I swear she opened up her eyes one more time to get a look at them. It seemed as if she were trying to squeeze their hands. My son wrote a poem about it and read it at her funeral.

We spent the night on Saturday night and cried inside as we listened to the gurgling noise she was now making trying to keep her body alive. It was the worst thing I had ever listened to. I try to forget those last few hours. Her mouth was bleeding from the sores from the drying air that was being forced into her lungs. Her eyes were still and crusty. I couldn't believe that I was sitting there hopelessly watching her as if I didn't realize who she was or what was going on right before my eyes. This is the woman I gauged my whole sense of self. If she didn't like what I was doing than I must be wrong. If she said it was the truth, then it must be the truth. I judged life from her very thoughts and feelings. My rights and wrongs were her rights and wrongs. If she said it, then it was what I should believe. I had never learned to think for myself. I was now forty nine years old and had never been able to make a decision on my own without first consulting her. Many a night I cried from bitter words that came from that swollen mouth. A part of me was dying. I had never learned how to cope without her opinion. Good or bad I had to know that I had her approval on everything that happened in my life. I mean everything.

So many things were going through my mind. I wasn't thinking about the release of now giving my family the respect that they deserved by being a mother and a wife. I was thinking only of how I was going to cope without having her thoughts and opinions. Even though I was a rebel for leaving the daycare, I still respected her opinion that I was wrong and selfish. My feelings for Kyle were wrong in her eyes. I just knew that someday I would have to pay for those feelings even though I knew that I had done nothing wrong by feeling the way I felt. I had asked God's forgiveness. I had never hurt Kyle, and always respected him, but I detested him greatly. Mom always brought shame on us when we didn't agree with her. Then she would say, *"I hope you ask God to forgive you for what you just said or did."* I thought, "If something happens to her, how will I know if I have the correct guilt and shame that I truly can't grasp on my own?" I know this sounds crazy, but it was true. I lived her every word.

It was quite in the hospital room as Janice and I kept our secret thoughts to ourselves, speaking only to see if one of us needed to eat or go to the restroom. Kyle was not there and we had forty-eight hours with our mother without the gloom that he always brought into the room. It was the greatest freedom we had ever experienced. If only she could say, "I love you" and "I am proud of you." What a release that would have been for both of us. Our hearts were heavy with pain and guilt. Yet we were sad to lose the one person that we adored so much. I can still hear her say, *"I shouldn't have to say I love you or I am proud of you. You should know that by now."* Did we? I didn't realize at the time that the only one I had to please was God. He is my Savior and he will truly be my judge when I am held up in a hospital room waiting for my final breathe to be taken. He is my glory and my hope for life everlasting. I learned a lot after her death.

The silence was broken at 3:00 in the afternoon as Kyle, Ron, Sarah and their families along with my uncle came bursting through the door. Kyle immediately took over and placed himself at the head of the bed asking us all kinds of questions. We gave him an account of all the events that had taken place for the last two days. Ron was loud as always and Sarah was tenderly talking to Mom as if she could understand her every word.

Janice and I took a break from all the confusion and went to the waiting room to eat lunch that our husbands had brought for us. My cousin, who is around my age, and his wife came in and sat with us before visiting Mom. We were eating and not really worried about returning to the room until the others left.

Around 6:00, Sarah came running down the hall and announced, "She's gone."

I was furious! "Why didn't you come and get us if you thought her breathing had changed? Couldn't you tell?"

Sarah started crying and Sarah said, "I came as soon as I noticed." All I could say is, "Oh, mama! Oh, mama!" I cried and cried and yet I had no feeling inside. Truth be known, she died when she lost consciousness. Why did she wait until we left the room? Why couldn't **we** be here when it happened? Oh God why? Everyone hugged each other and we stayed with her as long as we could before I had my husband call his father who was the mortician at the funeral home. Our husbands holding us, made us leave the room before they came to pick up the body. Kyle on the other hand, stayed until the very end. We all left and I felt as if I had been living a dream. My sister and her family along with the rest of their group gathered at my house. Once our dear friends heard the news, they brought their evening meal to my house. My father-in-law came over and we decided to meet with him and the other morticians at 11:00 the next morning. After everyone left I slipped into my bathroom and cried in the tub. It seemed like I didn't even close my eyes that night. The phone was ringing as I looked up at the clock and realized that it was almost time for our meeting. It was my father-in-law. He was wondering if he could come by and get a picture and an obituary to put in the paper. I said sure and called Janice. She said, "Go ahead and write one and I will be over as soon as I get dressed."

I was still in my gown when the door opened and standing

there with a gentleman from the funeral home was my father-in-law. He was asking me for a picture of Mom. I knew which one I wanted to use, but I had to clear it with the family. We didn't have much time, but I had made a picture of her at her birthday celebration and she had loved it. She even had me blow it up for her. Janice arrived and was in agreement with me. Kyle was not present and we called him to see if it was alright. He said, "Whatever" and we did what we could. Janice read the obituary and it sounded good to her. We gave him the information and he said we could change it if needed in the meeting. They took the picture and placed the information in the newspaper. When we arrived at the funeral home, Kyle was there along with Ron, Sarah, and my uncle, who now was his buddy and turned against us girls. This had been a close uncle. He had been there for us girls when Daddy died. He had supported us on the ball field. He took us to the fair. Taught us how to ski and camp. It was so sad that we lost so much when Mom died. Kyle spread all kind of lies to him in hopes that he too would take his side against us girls, and it worked.

The mortician in charge started gathering the information. He read what I had written and asked if there were to be any changes. No one said a thing at that time, but later Kyle made changes after we left. He was not happy with the picture I chose either. We picked out a coffin and then returned to see what things we wanted to do at the funeral. The mortician asked Kyle if she had life insurance.

He replied, "I don't know."

Janice said "Yes, she did have life insurance somewhere." He continued the questioning by asking the amount.

Kyle said, "I don't know."

Janice asked him, "Didn't you have life insurance through your work?"

He looked stunned. He knew he did, but he wanted us girls to pay for the funeral. I think she even agreed to help him look for it. He was so coy about the whole situation. He said he might not have enough money to bury her with. What a joke! We left him there in that room to discuss the payment. Before we left, the mortician asked what we wanted to bury her in. We all knew about the dress and then the jewelry was mentioned. My father-in-law and the other gentleman suggested that we not put any kind of rings on her hands because they could be stolen. We agreed. This made Kyle furious. He wanted her rings and he thought that he would be able to snatch them if given the chance. We spoke not a word and followed the group to the nearby flower shop to get the flowers from our families. As we approached the parking lot, Sarah jumped out of the car and started telling us that Daddy wanted those rings on Violet's fingers. She was so mad that she started crying.

Janice calmly said, "Sarah, the rings are now ours and we can do whatever we want with them. Your dad may have say over everything else, but he will not get these rings." They were all mad. We went in to get flowers and we all could not decide on what we were going to get together so each family picked out a bunch of flowers. Kyle and Ron chose another florist. He said his friend would make some up for him. It seemed that Kyle knew the lady on a personal basis. We never figured out who she was and how he was connected to her.

Kyle couldn't stop with the ring thing. He called the beautician who was a long time friend of Mom, Janice and I. He asked her to tell us that Mom wanted her rings on her fingers.

She then called Janice and said, "Kyle wants me to do your Mom's hair. You know I was expecting to do it."

Janice agreed and then she told her how he wanted her to talk us girls into putting her rings on her hand. Janice told her the whole story. She didn't have to say much. This lady knew Mom for twenty years and she knew what she was putting up with on a daily basis with Kyle. She knew more than we did.

Janice called Kyle and told him that she had not forgotten the lost jewelry that we were looking for on the Sunday before mom died. "You are willed all the assets of the house and the belongings."

"We are willed her personal belongings. I know the jewelry is there somewhere."

It didn't take Kyle long to find the lost jewelry. He bought it to the funeral home and we agreed to put her rings on her hand, but remove them every night before the funeral home closed. Thanks to my father-in-law.

Kyle kept his distance from Janice and me. His family was

there each night sitting in the corner watching and taking notes. Our friends and family sat in one corner and mutual friends sat in the middle of the room. Kyle never had any true friends. That's why he had to enlist my uncle to be his best buddy. My Sunday school friends fixed lunch for us after the funeral and we all went to this fancy house where we brought food from the funeral home to be shared by all of Kyle's family and a few of our close friends. A minister friend did the funeral and we all agreed that Mom would have been pleased. We met as a family and told the Pastor things that we remembered about her. Each one of us had a favorite song and somehow we managed to get through the service. Of course Ron being a minister had to say something spiritual on his behalf.

We knew in our heart that Mom had given up her spirit and joined the Lord in Heaven. Her desire was to be with us, but what a pleasant environment Heaven is compared to this wicked world. I know Mom was much happier than her family who was now left behind angry and bitter.

In this verse Paul was writing to the Philippians telling them that it is very important for him to remain on earth to share the life of Christ and his promise of a reward in Heaven. When his work was over Paul was rewarded with eternity.

Mom's work was done here and she now deserved to live with Christ where there were no worldly trials.

Philippians 1:23,24
I am torn between the two: I desire to depart and be with Christ, which is better by far; but it is more necessary for you that I remain in the body.

The Ties That Did Not Bind

The night before the service everything started to come to a head. We were at the last hour of the visitation and personal friends were holding our hands and visiting with Janice and me. She was on one side of the room and I was on the other. We were talking with friends that we had not seen in years.

All of a sudden Ron decided to grab up flowers and start splitting them up. He was carrying flowers and big plants to his car and Janice looked over at me and said, "Where is he going?"

I said, "Home, I guess."

She followed after him and said, "Who gave you the right to take charge? We haven't even seen all of the flowers."

He responded, "Well, I was going to give these roses to Daddy, and I was going to take the big plants that the church gave me..."

And before he could finish she screamed, "I'll be so glad when this is all over and I can be rid of his damned family!"

Oh boy, she hated what she had said, but it was true. She spoke her heart and mine. I should have said the same thing or at least an Amen! No, she got all the glory and the brunt of the criticism. At the funeral the next day as I was passing out the instructions on how to get to my friend's house, Ron said he wouldn't be coming to eat with the family. I wanted to shout GOOD! I could see that his wife was not mad. She was rather friendly and said, "We will come if Ron does. After this big sendoff, Ron refused to talk to either of us. We felt obligated to go to graduation parties and invite them to Christmas lunch, but Ron was never the same. The secret was out. The family who worked so hard to pretend to love each other hated every moment of it and now other people knew. What would Mom have said?

After the funeral Janice asked Kyle if it would be alright to come over to the house and get Mom's personal belongings out of his way. He said he didn't even have her will. Janice didn't have one, but I had one. We told Kyle that he had a copy of it with his will. She even told him where he had put them. They were there on the last Sunday we spent with Mom. Kyle denied that he had Mom's will and so we told him that the only items we were going to take would be her clothing and jewelry, anything that was personal to Mom. Mom had a car in her name that she bought from her nephew. Kyle hated that car. He was very upset when she bought the car. She wanted a car that she could get in and out of. Kyle drove a truck and they had a van. Against his wishes she purchased the car. She put the car in her name and left Kyle out of the whole thing. We told him we would sign the car over to him and he could use the money to pay for the funeral.

We arrived at Mom's house around 1:00 in the afternoon. Kyle was waiting for us along with Sarah and my uncle who was now his "twin" stuck to the hip. He spoke not a word to my sister or me. We tried to be as upbeat as possible. We talked to Kyle, but he was so mad that we were there that he ignored our small talk and asked us what we wanted.

"We only want to help you clear out her clothes and take her personal items like her makeup and jewelry. That is the only thing willed to us."

Kyle stayed in the room and watched as we walked into Mom's big walk-in closet and started pulling out her clothes. Sarah was right behind us. She watched each item we touched. We offered her anything she wanted. She took a house coat and maybe a blouse or something. As we pulled the clothes off of the hanger, we folded them and placed them in boxes and put them in our cars to take to the Goodwill store. Kyle was truly upset with the fact that we were looking through her closet. Shoes and purses were packed into boxes as Sarah watched on and huffed and puffed not even trying to help us fold the clothes. Kyle should have been happy that we were taking things out of his way. Mom had old clothes stuffed into that closet from 1980. In the back of her closet was a safe that had not been opened in years. Kyle said, "I don't know the combination to that safe. I told him that it was in her Bible and if he would find it I would open the safe. He just stood there and rolled his eyes. I thought if this had been a big problem, why didn't he ask Mom before she died what was in the safe?" I walked into the living room and found her Bible. I took the combination to the closet and opened the safe. Nothing was in there except some old papers. I looked at the papers and saw that it was my parents' divorce papers. Sarah was right over my shoulder. I didn't hide the information but just kept reading. There was a letter in there from my dad's lawyer asking if he could get custody of me. It was the first time in my life that I had ever known that my Dad wanted me. The letter said,

> We know that the oldest child is now able to make up her mind about visitation; however, Ora would like to have a chance to spend more time with Linda Sue who is the younger of the two girls.

Mom was not in agreement since Daddy was not paying child support. I guess she was now denying him the rights to visit with me. Kyle wanted the papers and reached for them as I announced, "These are the divorce papers from our parents. Do you want to save them for any reason?"

He looked shocked and said, "I know there are other important papers in there." As I placed the divorce papers in a box and looked into the empty safe, I said, "Here go ahead and find them." I know that was my smart mouth talking, but he had it coming. After we finished throwing out old shoes and coats, the closet was empty. There were no treasures in the closet unless you would count old clothes and smelly shoes. After we finished the closet, we went into the bedroom and opened up her jewelry box. There we found draws of costume jewelry that we had sorted out on the Sunday we cleaned out her dresser drawers. I suggested that we just take the big box home and sort out the jewelry.

Kyle soon told us that we could have some of the jewelry but not the jewelry box. "I gave her that box and I am going to keep it." Sarah had now placed herself on the bed opening the drawers and dragging out pieces of jewelry that her Daddy gave Violet. It was of my opinion that Sarah had already gone into that box and sorted out everything she was going to take. By rights, all of it belonged to us. It didn't matter who gave it to her. If it was Mom's, it was personal and jewelry was in that category. I admit, I wanted to smack Sarah's hand, but Janice and I calmly let her pick out everything she thought "Daddy" gave her. "Daddy," didn't give her much of anything. I don't see how she could pick out so many

things. We didn't argue. I retrieved two old shoe boxes from the
garbage and loaded the costume jewelry into those two small
boxes.

I walked into the living room and took one last look. Again
Sarah was right behind me. I opened the side table where Mom
would store pictures that we would give her of our kids. School
pictures, Christmas and vacation pictures. I took the last stack of
pictures that I had given her of my family.

Sarah asked me to see what I was taking. She said, "Some of
them might be pictures I gave Daddy."

I assured her that they were of my family and I am sure her
'Daddy' doesn't want my pictures.

She replied, "Well, you don't know that."

I opened up the coffee table and saw Mom's Bible. "You think I
could have her Bible?"

Sarah was very angry now, "No! My grandparents gave that to
them when they got married."

I wanted to say, "It's a shame that your daddy doesn't read it.
If he had, he would have known the combination to the safe in the
closet."

I approached my Mom's desk to see if she had written any
personal notes that might be of any interest. Sarah told me that
there was no use even looking in there. All she has in that desk is
old Christmas cards and blank pieces of paper. I checked for
myself and Sarah was right. If there was anything in the desk it
was now gone.

As I walked through the dining room, I met my sister. She had
been asking Kyle if it was alright to take Mom's rolling pin that
she got for her first wedding shower when she was eighteen years
old. She was also debating him about the cookbooks that were
always in the kitchen drawer. He let her look and gave her what
she wanted, making sure that she only took what she asked for.

Sarah, on the other hand was watching me in the dining room.
Every dish I picked up she would tell me that she got that after
she married Daddy or my great aunt gave that to her. There
wasn't one dish that she would allow me to pick up without a
comment.

Finally, I took a pie dish I gave her and looked her straight in
the eye and now don't tell me that your aunt gave her this. Sarah

shrugged and I put it in the small box next to the shoe boxes.

I didn't get one tablecloth, not one piece of silver, stem of crystal or china. I took a cup with my boy's picture on it and left the dining room. There was no use to argue with these two mad bulls. I wanted out. Why would I want anything to remind me of this house of horrors?

As I walked back into the family room, I saw Mom's journals sitting next to her lift chair. I didn't even ask I just grabbed them before Kyle and Sarah told me to leave them alone. I didn't get all of them but I managed to grab four. She had a copy of this book that she was continuing. However, when I asked Kyle what happened to it, he said he didn't know that she was writing one. Boy, could he forget when he wanted. I do know that she wrote some unkind things about her marriage to him, but I could never find the book.

Janice cleared out her old makeup and found nothing of any interest in the bathroom. All evidence of a women living in the house had been deleted. It was now ready for him to start his new life. He didn't have to deal with cleaning out Mom's stuff. He should have been happy. He got the house, all the contents, the lake house, all its contents, the boats, the cars, the van, and a new truck. Gee, what more can you ask for? Weeks later he had a new car yet he was badmouthing us girls saying we had not given him the title to the car we promised him. He didn't realize that the will had not been probated and it took time after a death to change the names on deeds. My sister and I were furious that he would tell church people that we refused to give him the deed to her car. After all it was in her name and we were willed the car. As soon as time allowed, we pulled some strings with my nephew that is a lawyer and got him the car sooner than we should have. He didn't even say thank you! He even had my uncle badmouthing us telling people that were close friends that we were trying to keep his car away from him. What lies!

The hurt continued as weeks and months passed. We felt guilty not spending time with them on holidays. We made plans to eat lunch together and get him gifts. Soon I learned that the guilt trip was not necessary. They had already planned Easter, Thanksgiving and Christmas together without even considering us. We all wanted away from each other. I did visit Sarah's house for a graduation party for her son and saw many of the things that were in Mom's house, her desk, folding table and chairs, her cat that sat next to the fireplace, and much more. I was hurt, but I had to move on with my feelings. These were only things. Things were not going to bring back my Mother. Things were never going to bring love to my heart that I never had.

My feelings for Sarah, Ron, and Kyle were digging into my soul. How could I be a good Christian if I didn't forgive? I found out that Kyle was moving. He was selling all of Mom's things and moving into a smaller house. I talked to him on the phone and asked where he was moving. He said somewhere out there by the Dairy Queen. He never gave me an address. He then gave me his new phone number, but mixed his numbers up. I still didn't get it. I was feeling guilty that I should maybe go visit. What was I thinking? He was reluctant to tell Janice what price he got out of the house.

He told her "Well, okay, I guess you will see it in the newspaper." We still didn't get it. Janice was calling him to tell him what was going on, and I invited him to my son's graduation and graduation party. He showed up for the party but didn't speak but a few words to me. He was telling everyone that we would not go see him, yet I had asked him several times to call me and invite me to his house. I told him we would be glad to visit. I have yet to get that call. You see again, I still didn't get it! Mom had put such guilt in us concerning Kyle that we thought that we **had** to make him a part of our lives. He wanted his freedom and **we didn't get it!**

The Christmas after Mom died, the funeral home held a service for all of the families that had lost loved ones in 2003. Kyle was notified and of course he never invited us to attend. This was a hard year on all of us. A service together could have helped us accept the departure of the family. It never happened. His hate for us was deep.

More and more anger was building in my heart and Janice's heart. Once again we were shut out of a family. We had no say with our father and now the same was happening with Mom.

After several sessions with a therapist, I learned that I never again in my life had to deal with any of that side of the family. In fact it would be better for me mentally and physically to let go of all the memories. Put the past in the closet and shut the door. Put a chair in front of the door. I was getting it, but I confess that I still peek into the closed door from time to time. I was doing pretty well until Christmas when Kyle stopped by my house to give us twenty dollars. He was all sad and said he went to the graveyard every day. I later learned that those tears were for my benefit. Two hours later he was taking his girlfriend to a Christmas Eve service at his church. Oh yes! I forgot to mention that he had a girlfriend soon after Mom died. They tried to keep it a secret from us but too many people saw them together. They still sit apart at church on Sundays so it looks like he is grieving for Mom.

Although God permits Satan to work in our world, God is still in control. Jesus, because He is God, has power over Satan. Jesus is able to drive out demons and end their terrible work in people's lives.

I have to forgive to be a Christian. I must forgive but I don't have to open the door for more conflicts and non-Christian attitudes.

Mark 3:24
If a house is divided against itself, that house cannot stand.

Happiness is Knowing That Jesus Christ Loves You!

Violet had a lifetime of abuse. She wanted to love and be loved. Her love of life and the freedom to escape into the world of acceptance was deflated. I truly believe that my Mom would have been a different person if she was given the permission she needed to just be herself. She never learned to love Violet. She broke away from her abusive father at the age of eighteen. She looked forward to a life of happiness. She loved Ora, and not only was he her ticket out of the family, but he was the love of her life. He made her laugh. He took her places that she had never been before. He found her attractive and exciting. There was something inside of him that allowed her to open up and express herself in a way she never knew she could. This would be something she would hang on to for the rest of her life. The little bits of happiness that snuck into the marriage were not worth giving up. All the fights, the abuse and the rejection could be ignored if only he would come back and bring the initial feeling of excitement and goose bumps she felt when they first met. She never stopped thinking about him.

When she got married to Kyle, she had to prove to Ora that she was worthy of someone's love and affection. She had to prove that she was successful. Everything she did from that time on was to prove to Ora that she had worth. She talked about him nonstop. Sometimes she would share good things about him, other times she would angrily lash out at him for leaving her and ruining our family. I believe there was always hope in her heart that they would someday be together. If there was any hope at all, it was lost the day he died. She would now have to settle for Kyle and the lack of love that he brought to the marriage. She confessed several times that she never loved Kyle like she did Daddy.

I believe that Mom was never happy with her second marriage.

The last few years of her life were spent with so much bitterness that she turned against all of us who truly tried to reach out to her. We wanted for mom to live life to the fullest. Look for happiness in each day. She woke with a vengeance in the morning and all the antidepressants and nerve pills prescribed could not alter her broken heart that brought emptiness to her life.

Kyle would do anything she asked him to do. He might fuss about it for a while, but you can bet that he would get up at any hour to get her anything she wanted. She held that in high esteem. She was proud that he would take care of her by doing what she wanted. She became so dependent on him that she didn't know how to do things for herself. He ran to the store, bank, drugstore, or restaurant to get her the most bizarre items at the oddest time of day or night. Even though Kyle was serving her, he enjoyed his little trips away from the house. When Mom stopped driving, she gave up her freedom. She put on a good show. She loved to tell everyone that he was wonderful to her. She never explained that she paid a huge price for all that attention. She took care of his family and gave him money for everything.

Kyle's problem was his attitude. He was a total downer. He looked for something to go wrong every second of the day. If she said something was good he would find fault in it. I never left the house without him telling me that I better stop and look before I backed out of the drive. He would shout "I just know that a car will come down the street and hit you one of these days." To my surprise it never happened. When Mom cooked he would tell her that she was going to burn something on the stove. If she was cooking when he came in from the outside, he would call out, "Something's burning!" We would all come running to find out that once again he was crying wolf. If Mom was lifting something out of the cabinet he would say, "Look out! Everything is going to fall out and hit you on the head." He watched her every move. He criticized her every breathing moment. He turned her into a bitter person who found no reason to get up in the morning. He turned her against us. Now after her death he lies to friends telling them that we took all of her stuff out of the house the day after she was buried. Angry words that are meant to put us in an unfavorable light. If people really knew what our relationship was like. If he had been a caring loving stepfather, he would have said, "Girls, is there anything here you want of your mother's?" He would have included us in on the selling of the house. He never told us. We heard it from family friends. We could have given him money for things that he took over to the flea market to sell. Instead it was all done in secret. He has never to this day invited any of our family over to his house. This shows his loyalty to mom and her daughters.

Mom died on March 23, 2003. It so happened that my Dad died on March 24 1967. They were also born a day apart from each other. Mom was born January 12 and Daddy was born January 13. Two people who met and by chance gave birth to two little girls looking for happiness and a normal family. We loved them both yet they hurt us in so many ways. Janice and I have a lot of healing to do. Fortunately the one thing Mom encouraged was faith in Jesus Christ. We both left the church where we felt bondage by memories of Mom and Kyle. It was the smartest thing we ever did. God guided us away from the church long before Mom passed away. I can see now that it was in His great scheme of things. We have Christian friends who love the Lord and have become our new family. It's like starting life all over again. I have learned to love the Lord and turn to His Word for my every need. I know that Grace is something that God has given me as a gift. I must forgive Mom, Daddy and Kyle. I know that there is someone that loves me, accepts me, and assures me daily that I am worthy of His promise of life after death.

God has plans for Janice and me. He uses us to help others in need. Even though our life was never what we wanted, we are in God's plan.

I know that God will use me and my experiences in a positive way. I must have faith. I must go on with my life. I must close the door to past hurts. God holds me tightly together so the cracked and broken pieces of my life can heal. I only wish my Mother could have experienced the same freedom.

I know Violet's love for Christ influenced many people. I will always thank her for making God a part of our lives. I know God had a plan for her life. She raised two orphaned children. She influenced the lives of children in her daycare center. She taught children in church about the love of Jesus. She gave away money to those in need.

She came from nothing, but became wealthy using her creative talents to become a pioneer in the field of childcare. She never let anything stand in her way. God was her partner, and although she left this world discouraged and unhappy, you can never say she was a failure. She will always be remembered by those that loved her as Miss Violet a warm, wonderful woman who cared for everyone. She was a woman who had the gift of giving. A woman who wanted everyone to go to church and live for Christ. Her faith was never a secret. She shared her success with those she met. Everyone in town knew her kindness toward those in need both spiritually and physically.

She writes the following statement in her life story and the pastor read it at her funeral,

I am at home and retired. Can't say I like it, but I am glad I can stay here and still make money. I can enjoy my grandchildren. They are the most wonderful, biggest blessing anyone can have. I even have time for Benji the dog. They are my shining stars. I love my church and all my friends there. I have loved all our pastors and they have been at home in my house. I wanted to set good examples for my children. I want all of my children and grandchildren to be the best Christians they can and work in the church. Accept Jesus and take your families to church. I want to someday see all of my children and grandchildren in heaven.

Now you can understand why her story had to be told. She was no ordinary woman.

About the Author

LS King is a native of Louisville, Kentucky. She graduated from University of Louisville where she earned a masters degree in education. Mrs. King loves to write true stories about phenomenal people and events. Her first two books, *No Ordinary Woman* and *Lady Bray* are examples of strong women who overcame adversity at the turn of the 20th Century. The books are not only entertaining but paint a historical view of the time the characters grew up in.

Her books also reflect her strong faith in God, with the new book *Divine Interventions* portraying actual events that happened in Mrs. King's life and the lives of people she knows. From graduating college, to teaching school, to being nominated as one of Louisville's phenomenal women in 2001, Mrs. King hopes her books will be an inspiration and blessing to all who read them.

www.ingramcontent.com/pod-product-compliance
Lightning Source LLC
Chambersburg PA
CBHW051954090426
42741CB00008B/1395